Planning for IPv6

Silvia Hagen

Beijing · Cambridge · Farnham · Köln · Sebastopol · Tokyo

Planning for IPv6
by Silvia Hagen

Copyright © 2011 Silvia Hagen. All rights reserved.
Printed in the United States of America.

Published by O'Reilly Media, Inc., 1005 Gravenstein Highway North, Sebastopol, CA 95472.

O'Reilly books may be purchased for educational, business, or sales promotional use. Online editions are also available for most titles (*http://my.safaribooksonline.com*). For more information, contact our corporate/institutional sales department: (800) 998-9938 or *corporate@oreilly.com*.

Editors: Mike Loukides and Meghan Blanchette	**Cover Designer:** Karen Montgomery
Production Editor: Kristen Borg	**Interior Designer:** David Futato
Copyeditor: Rachel Monaghan	**Illustrator:** Robert Romano

ISBN: 978-1-449-30539-0

[LSI]

1315323542

Table of Contents

Preface

Many readers may be awaiting the third edition of *IPv6 Essentials*. The event on February 3, 2011, when the IANA (Internet Assigned Numbers Authority) finally announced the depletion of the global IPv4 address pool changed the world. People seemed to wake up and realize it was high time to start planning for IPv6. But where to start?

So we decided to wait to update *IPv6 Essentials* (since it is really not that outdated) and instead provide a book to help with this planning. After all, before you need the bits and bytes of the protocol, you need to do some planning.

In this book, I try to put everything I have learned in more than 10 years of studying, working, playing, teaching, and consulting with IPv6 at your disposal—everything that is relevant to help you understand what it takes to plan the integration of IPv6. The book is basically a summary of all the answers to the most frequent questions I get when talking with customers. And I hope it also makes you feel a little enthusiastic about the opportunities that IPv6 offers. So, with that, I wish you a good read and lots of fun learning about and planning for IPv6.

Audience

This book is written for anyone who is interested in learning how to best plan for the integration of IPv6 in an enterprise. The larger the network, the more complex the task—adding a new transport protocol affects every single network component. You don't have to be a tech-geek to love this book (although if you are, I hope you love it too). It is more about what it takes to introduce IPv6 in an enterprise, written for CTOs, decision makers, IT managers, people who architect and design networks, and people who will be leading IPv6 projects, as well as for all the members of the planning team.

About This Book

Many of the challenges you will face are on the nontechnical, organizational level. Having worked with large enterprises for many years, I know how difficult it can sometimes be to get all the different IT groups around one table and have them talk and listen to each other—and this is exactly what you will have to do to plan for IPv6. This book covers IPv6-specific topics so you understand what is involved in the process, as well as what questions you will have to ask to develop a high-level strategy. Planning for a successful integration is more about asking the right questions than finding quick answers.

What this book will *not* give you is a "one-size-fits-all" strategy. As you will understand after reading this book, there is no single best way that fits every organization. Each network is different, each organization is unique, and there are so many different aspects that factor into the planning that each path from today's IPv4-dominant network to an IPv6-dominant network is unique also.

Assumptions This Book Makes

This book assumes that you have a good understanding of IT and technology projects. It doesn't replace education and experience in project planning; it outlines only what is specific to planning for IPv6. You should have some general understanding of networking concepts and IPv4 networks. You don't necessarily need a lot of understanding of IPv6, although it makes all the discussions more meaningful if you do.

Contents of This Book

This book is organized into three chapters:

Chapter 1, The Business Case
> This chapter discusses the business case and has two target groups. You may be insecure because of all the contradictory information you hear, and about the common belief that IPv6 has no business case. I discuss this issue in a larger context, which usually resolves the contradictions. This chapter can also be helpful if you know that introducing IPv6 is business-critical, but you need arguments to convince your boss or your business partners. An important part of this chapter covers the opportunities IPv6 offers. Instead of focusing on the pains and risks of IPv6, it is much more helpful to understand the opportunities it presents so you can make best use of its potential. You are building your next-generation network, after all.

Chapter 2, Planning for IPv6

This chapter covers the planning itself, starting with tasks that should be performed in advance and then moving on to creating a high-level design and conducting a network assessment, how to evaluate vendors and products, and how to build labs and test. It also describes some general decisions and considerations you will face when defining your high-level implementation plan, such as routing protocol choices, security designs, DNS issues to understand, how to create an IPv6 address plan and how to manage IPv6 addresses.

Chapter 3, Integration and Transition Technologies

This chapter provides a high-level discussion of the available integration and transition technologies. It is not intended to be an in-depth technical guide. The technologies are described in an overview so you can clearly understand what is available and when to use these mechanisms.

Conventions Used in This Book

The following typographical conventions are used in this book:

Italic

Indicates new terms, URLs, email addresses, filenames, and file extensions.

`Constant width`

Used for program listings, as well as within paragraphs to refer to program elements such as variable or function names, databases, data types, environment variables, statements, and keywords.

`Constant width bold`

Shows commands or other text that should be typed literally by the user.

`Constant width italic`

Shows text that should be replaced with user-supplied values or by values determined by context.

This icon signifies a tip, suggestion, or general note.

This icon indicates a warning or caution.

Using Code Examples

This book is here to help you get your job done. In general, you may use the code in this book in your programs and documentation. You do not need to contact us for permission unless you're reproducing a significant portion of the code. For example, writing a program that uses several chunks of code from this book does not require permission. Selling or distributing a CD-ROM of examples from O'Reilly books does require permission. Answering a question by citing this book and quoting example code does not require permission. Incorporating a significant amount of example code from this book into your product's documentation does require permission.

We appreciate, but do not require, attribution. An attribution usually includes the title, author, publisher, and ISBN. For example: "*Planning for IPv6* by Silvia Hagen (O'Reilly). Copyright 2011 Silvia Hagen, 978-1-449-30539-0."

If you feel your use of code examples falls outside fair use or the permission given above, feel free to contact us at *permissions@oreilly.com*.

Safari® Books Online

Safari Books Online is an on-demand digital library that lets you easily search over 7,500 technology and creative reference books and videos to find the answers you need quickly.

With a subscription, you can read any page and watch any video from our library online. Read books on your cell phone and mobile devices. Access new titles before they are available for print, and get exclusive access to manuscripts in development and post feedback for the authors. Copy and paste code samples, organize your favorites, download chapters, bookmark key sections, create notes, print out pages, and benefit from tons of other time-saving features.

O'Reilly Media has uploaded this book to the Safari Books Online service. To have full digital access to this book and others on similar topics from O'Reilly and other publishers, sign up for free at *http://my.safaribooksonline.com*.

How to Contact Us

Please address comments and questions concerning this book to the publisher:

O'Reilly Media, Inc.
1005 Gravenstein Highway North
Sebastopol, CA 95472
800-998-9938 (in the United States or Canada)
707-829-0515 (international or local)
707-829-0104 (fax)

We have a web page for this book, where we list errata, examples, and any additional information. You can access this page at:

http://oreilly.com/catalog/9781449305390

To comment or ask technical questions about this book, send email to:

bookquestions@oreilly.com

For more information about our books, courses, conferences, and news, see our website at *http://www.oreilly.com*.

Find us on Facebook: *http://facebook.com/oreilly*

Follow us on Twitter: *http://twitter.com/oreillymedia*

Watch us on YouTube: *http://www.youtube.com/oreillymedia*

Acknowledgments

I would like to thank everybody who has supported my work for IPv6 over the years. There are many wonderful people in the global IPv6 community, and it is always a pleasure to meet at one of the conferences and share information and experience. I like to call them the IPv6 family. For the content in this book, I thank all my customers and students, who keep challenging me again and again with new questions that make me look for new answers. They are the ones that keep me awake, continuously expanding my horizons. Specifically for this book, I thank the people who have helped shape it by reviewing and providing feedback. They are Fred Wettling, Bechtel Corporation, Ciprian Popoviciu, Nephos6, Andrew Yourtchenko, Rich Hardenstein and Cello Klebl.

I'd also like to thank my editor at O'Reilly, Mike Loukides, for asking for this book and providing a perfect platform to bring this information to the market in a very timely manner. And to all the wonderful and supportive people on the production team who make working with O'Reilly as an author a good experience.

The Business Case

In this first chapter, I'll discuss the business case and try to put it in a larger context than usual to open the discussion for new perspectives and opportunities. Resolving the business case discussions and putting the integration of IPv6 in the right context paves the way for you to actually focus on the demands of planning for a successful integration.

Many people hesitate to start the planning phase, probably because it often seems to be an insurmountable task, with challenges that are way too complex to even start thinking about it.

While it is true that integration in a larger network is not a no-brainer and takes a lot of time and careful planning, there is no need to panic or think that you can't handle it. Every decent engineer who mastered the introduction of DHCP, VPNs, and NATs will also master the introduction of IPv6. The difference is that IPv6, as the transport protocol, touches every component in the network, so the complexity of integrating it comes from having to consider all the interactions between the different network components and services.

But the process can be broken down into single, doable steps, and you don't have to complete them in three months if you start early enough. This book provides an outline to help you determine how you want to go about tackling it.

The Inevitable Business Case Discussion

The discussion around the lack of a business case for IPv6 is historically the most used good reason to avoid integrating IPv6. The root of this argument seems to lie in the combination of misunderstandings and a lack of context.

A business case addresses, at a high level, the business need that the project seeks to meet. It addresses the reasons for the project, the expected business benefits and risks, the options considered, and the expected costs of the project.

To define a business case, you must specify the parameters that qualify it, and what constitutes a valuable business case may differ depending on the corporate culture. In other words, what might qualify as a substantial business case in one corporate culture may not be considered a business case in another culture because the corporate values are different.

In general, we can say that IPv6 is part of evolving our infrastructure, evolving the network that transports all data— it is the future highway for our data. So asking for a business case for IPv6 is like asking for the business case of running a network. But running our businesses without using scalable, high performance networks is not really an option anymore. So there is not much choice, we must continue to invest in evolving our networks, just like we have done since the early days of running networks; otherwise, they will stop providing useful services for our businesses and hinder our competitiveness at some point in the near future.

The Human Capacity for Predictions and the Business Case of Evolution

Our business case calculations and the common opinion that IPv6 has no business case are based on expectations and predictions. What we think will be happening in three to five years is what we base our judgments on.

If we look at history, though, we see that our capacity for accurate predictions is pretty limited. Back in the early 1980s, studies were conducted to determine the likelihood that in the future there would be a computer on every desk of an organization. The results showed that this was very unlikely. But only a few years later, a computer on every desk was a reality, and soon people often had not just one, but multiple computers.

In the early 1990s, studies showed that it was highly unlikely that everyone would soon have a cell phone. After all, the early versions were heavy and looked like sewing machines. Only a few years later, however, schools had to prevent students from using their cell phones during lectures and exams because they were using them to exchange results with each other. And at the same time, nobody spotted the business case for SMS (text messages). It was mainly a leftover from development, and it simply wasn't removed from production. Yet, SMS hit the world, became widely used overnight, and today is making gigantic profits for many organizations.

So are we good at making predictions and determining business cases? Obviously not. Did someone foresee the emergence and success of Google, Skype, Facebook, and Twitter? Was there a careful business case defined before these technologies were developed? It seems that services can become very successful even if we haven't thought about a business case beforehand; and in fact, had the developers tried to make a business case for the aforementioned technologies, they may well have arrived at the conclusion that there wasn't one and opted not to deploy the service.

This is how evolution works. Technology and science are an expression of the evolution of human consciousness. And because this is a collective factor, it is highly unpredictable. In the 1920s, for instance, it was a huge problem that more and more people were starting to use horses for transport. Initially, only the rich could afford traveling by horse, but soon everyone was using them. Trend analysts predicted that mankind would soon drown in horse dung. This was a serious concern, and nobody could think of a useful answer to this problem. The solution came from a very unexpected angle. It was the invention of the car, and it revolutionized not only the transportation system, but also the whole industry. This example confirms Albert Einstein's assertion that "no problem can be solved from the same level of consciousness that created it." Now we face new problems that have emerged from the invention of the car, and just like with the horse dung dilemma, we don't really know how to solve them. Chances are, the true solution will come from an unexpected evolutionary angle again.

For the car to be used widely, we needed better streets. Today we have an extended high-level street system in large parts of the world to enable transport for all the cars in use. Was there a business case for building all these streets? I guess nobody asked the question in this way; otherwise, we would probably not have our current street system.

Some creative developers designed IPv4 in the early 1970s. Their goal was to develop a protocol to connect a handful of computers. They managed to create a protocol that is the basic transport for our gigantic modern-day Internet (approximately 2 billion users in 2011, growing exponentially; up from 360 million in 2001). But these developers did not have anything like the Internet in mind. There was no business plan and no business case for the Internet. It just happened during the 1990s; the world picked it up and started using it on a widespread scale, from online ecommerce in the mid-1990s to today's social networking and cloud services. And the IETF (Internet Engineering Task Force) responded to the market demand and developed all the extensions to IPv4 that we currently use.

 There was no business case for the Internet because *evolution doesn't need a business case.* Evolution just happens without asking us.

And by the way, don't think this is the end—evolution is also never-ending. For example, Vint Cerf, the "father of the Internet," and one of the guys who developed IPv4 in those early days, is now working on standardizing the Interplanetary Communication protocol based on the Bundle Protocol (RFC 5050); first implementations are currently available and tests are being run. So, while we may think this sounds crazy because we're focused on planetary issues like danger from atomic power, natural catastrophes, wars, and financial crisis, some visionaries are working on the future— with no business case, but fueled by evolutionary impulses.

The Internet has definitely reshaped our world, changed the way we communicate, impacted the way we approach business and education, broken down hierarchies, and established an important ingredient for globalization. It happened because we all jumped on the bandwagon, saw it as a useful tool, and started investing and participating in building and extending it. It is a global collective collaboration.

So what is the business case for IPv6? If you want, we can put it like this:

> The business case for IPv6 is the continued use and expansion of the Internet.

Without the introduction of IPv6, the Internet cannot continue to grow now that the IPv4 address space is definitely exhausted. This means that everyone who uses and profits from the Internet has to do his part in helping integrate IPv6. Integration too will have to be a global collective collaboration. For some corporate cultures, this might be a sufficient business case.

But let's go on and analyze the business case question in detail in a more practical context.

IPv6 Has No Immediate Business Case for Many

Corporations and organizations have maintained networks for many years. When we started maintaining them, mostly in the early 1990s, the networks were small and few were the tools we had available to manage them. Soon the number of network devices and the variety of network services were growing exponentially. At the same time, the requirements for management, administration, and security were increasing. When we started designing our IPv4-based networks, we did not have a real understanding of what lay ahead. But we learned while growing the networks and whenever we faced new challenges, we finally found solutions; and when public demand became obvious, the IETF developed all the useful extensions to the IPv4 protocol, such as DNS, DHCP, IPSec, and NAT.

With regard to the business case, we can say that the evolution, extension, and optimization of our network infrastructure always came at a cost. In other words, evolving our network has always been part of our returning budget—costs used to maintain a state-of-the-art infrastructure capable of running state-of-the-art services. We have to extend our infrastructure for more bandwidth constantly, as the services running on top continue to consume more bandwidth. We have to replace network devices in regular cycles, and when it comes to replacing core routers, this is usually a substantial cost factor. We also have to invest a lot into securing our networks and providing an infrastructure that can accommodate the demands of mobile users. And we constantly upgrade operating systems to newer versions, such as the currently ongoing migration from Windows Server 2003 to Windows Server 2008.

Do all these investments have a business case? What is the business case in upgrading a core router? What is the business case in upgrading a server operating system? Both do their job—they route or run services—so why should we invest in upgrading them?

The business case is not in the router or in the operating system. But we know that if we don't upgrade to a current version, the devices or operating systems will perform poorly or fail at some point, or we won't be able to run new services on top of them. This is a common case for Windows servers; Microsoft does a good job of keeping us all busy with constant upgrades by developing services and applications that don't run on older infrastructures.

Prudent investments in networking and other infrastructure are not just an expense—they often result in improved capabilities and a foundation for future innovation. Public cost of network capacity per megabit has continued to drop over time, enabling new services such as broadband video and distributed high-performance computing. And another important point to note is that all these investments can only make sense when viewed with a perspective longer than just six months or a year.

Likewise, IPv6 is not an application or a service that needs a business case. It is part of our infrastructure, it is the highway over which we can run our services, just as routers are part of that highway. So the introduction of IPv6 is the next natural step in evolving our infrastructure to be compatible with new services. And I guarantee that applications and services will be developed that will run only on an IPv6 network, because they use new features of the protocol that cannot be run on an IPv4 network. Microsoft has already started that trend by delivering DirectAccess as part of a Windows 7 license, which provides VPN functionality at no extra cost but uses IPv6 exclusively.

So the business case is not in IPv6, the business case is in applications and services that will soon require IPv6, or need so many IP addresses that IPv4 can't handle them anymore. And by the way, don't wait until your customers ask for IPv6, because they probably never will. They will ask for services, and those services might just happen to require an IPv6 infrastructure. Or your CEO may suddenly ask for a new and cool ecommerce application, or a new collaboration tool that happens to use IPv6 features—and he'll probably want it implemented in three months.

Integrating IPv6 under time pressure creates many disadvantages. High costs and unnecessary risks are the consequences. You lose the opportunity to learn as you go, to carefully plan, evaluate and test. By integrating IPv6 you lay the foundation for your next generation network. Take your time to do it carefully. By delaying the adoption of IPv6 for too long, you are putting your company's competitiveness at risk.

The integration of IPv6 in a more complex network can take three to five years if you want to do it in a risk-free and digestible way, with enough time to carefully build, secure, and manage a robust network and educate your team before that network encounters critical user traffic. You shouldn't wait until your customer or your CEO asks for these IPv6 applications.

IPv6 Has an Immediate Business Case for Some

There are also several sound, leading indicators that IPv6 is part of our future, specifically in the areas of standards that require IPv6 for the delivery of new services. Based on the industry-developed standards, new services are starting to emerge in the areas of content delivery, mobility, and industrial networking.

- The most current versions of *all* major computer operating systems have IPv6 installed and enabled by default.
- IMS (IP-Multimedia Subsystem) was originally developed by the mobile broadband standard organization 3GPP. IMS was designed to deliver Internet protocol multimedia service to mobile users, and has been adopted as a core component within cellular, fixed telecoms, and cable network providers. It requires IPv6 support. The seamless delivery of voice, data and video through IMS has been adopted my many of the international cellular LTE network and handset providers to address increased content variety, reliability, availability, and service quality. Companies that are stuck on proprietary convergence protocols may end up at a competitive disadvantage. Content providers are tuning their systems to more easily supply services over IMS-based networks.
- DOCSIS 3. 0 (Data Over Cable Service Interface Specification version 3.0), developed by CableLabs, is enabling traditional cable television operators to deliver a full spectrum of voice, data, and video services at previously impossible levels. IPv6 support is required in the DOCSIS 3.0 specifications. Implementation of DOCSIS 3.0 gives cable companies a competitive advantage over legacy wired broadband providers, enabling them to offer services ranging from VoIP to multiband, high-definition television to Internet speeds over 100 Mbps through channel bonding.
- The "Internet of Things" is becoming a reality with new IPv6-based standards supporting massive deployments of IPv6 RF sensor networks, such as the millions of Pacific Gas and Electric (PG&E) smart electrical meters.

IPv6 is enabled on the computers we are buying and the services we will depend on. There may be no immediate return on investment (ROI) for your organization, but failure to act now may leave some organizations in the land of yesterday, unable to compete or operate efficiently going forward.

What You Lose If You Don't Invest in IPv6

We can turn the business case question around and ask: what do we lose if we don't invest in and plan for IPv6?

- We will face extra costs and risks due to having an outdated infrastructure. Managing, securing, and extending an IPv4 infrastructure will become more and more costly, and state-of-the-art applications with high-performance requirements may not work well.

- We may not be able to integrate new applications and services because they may require IPv6 features and won't work in an IPv4 network.
- We can lose markets and customers due to outdated services. If we wait too long, we put our company's competitiveness at risk.
- We may not be able to introduce new services because they require an unusually high number of IP addresses (for instance, sensor and remote control systems being developed in many different industries including health care, automotive industry, disaster prevention, and many others).
- We may soon have limited global connectivity because now that the IPv4 address space is exhausted, Internet growth will happen over IPv6.
- We may not be able to communicate with newer customers, partners, and suppliers that are on new IPv6-only networks.
- Customers expecting or demanding IPv6-compatible or IPv6-enabled products and services may turn to our competitors for their needs. This possibility is acutely reflected in the 2009 update to the procurement requirements of the United States Federal Acquisition Regulation, which stipulates that "Internet Protocol Version 6 (IPv6) compliant products be included in all new information technology (IT) acquisitions using Internet Protocol (IP)."
- If we wait until time pressure is high, we will lose the opportunity to integrate IPv6 with careful planning and with a step-by-step integration. High risks and unnecessary costs are associated with this approach—not only unnecessary costs in deployment, but also unnecessary and recurring operational costs for the administration of a poorly designed network. The step-by-step approach provides the opportunity to learn as we go and to take advantage of lessons learned.

For long-term business planning, it's important to note that any investment in IPv4 is an investment in an end-of-life technology and must be migrated at some point. An investment in IPv6 is an investment in future technology. And yes, in the beginning it is more difficult, because we have to build knowledge and experience, but we'll eventually have to do this anyway. So why not start today?

Where Does Time Pressure Come From?

It is still a widely held perception that there is no immediate pressure to migrate to IPv6. There's also a persistent misbelief that if you have enough IPv4 addresses for your corporate devices, you don't need to integrate IPv6, even as of February 3, 2011, the date on which the depletion of the global IANA IPv4 address pool was announced.

So let's look at the situations that can create time pressure for you. Anticipating these situations will help you plan your integration accordingly so you can avoid having to deploy IPv6 without adequate preparation.

Lack of IPv4 addresses

Even if you think you still have enough IPv4 addresses, this can change upon a closer analysis. On one hand, more and more applications and services need always-on IP connectivity. On the other hand, enterprise environments consist of more and more overlays running on the same infrastructure. Desktop access, WLAN access, VoIP service, thin client, environment instrumentation (sensors), business specific services (healthcare devices). Each overlay needs its own IP address space and structure to simplify operations, yet this implies a less efficient use of the internal address space. These factors led several organizations to run out of the private IPv4 address space (RFC 1918) today. Also, if you want to introduce IPv6 with the *dual-stack approach*, where devices need both an IPv4 and an IPv6 address, it will work only if you implement it while you still have enough IPv4 addresses. While IPv4 addresses are still available internally, the dual-stack approach can ensure that both IPv4-only and IPv6-only sites and services are reachable from the enterprise's network natively, without disruption and without the potential problems of a NAT or translation-based services between endpoints.

When a customer or your CEO wants a new application or service that requires IPv6

If new applications make use of IPv6's advanced features (such as extension headers) or Mobile IPv6's advanced features, they will not run on an IPv4 network. So if you have a strong business requirement to introduce such an application, you might face a critical situation if you have not prepared for IPv6. This scenario will force you to integrate IPv6 without the necessary preparation, an optimal address plan design, or the required understanding of networking, security, and management concepts specific to IPv6. And you will have production traffic on an IPv6 network that you didn't have enough time to test thoroughly.

Internet growth

From the day on which the IPv4 space is definitely depleted—which already happened in the APNIC region and will be happening sometime in 2011 for the ARIN and RIPE region—Internet growth will mostly be IPv6-only. Because of the quickly increasing number of Internet users with IPv6-only Internet access, your reach is limited if you support only IPv4. You could use translation and NAT techniques (and ISPs will probably do this due to lack of alternatives), but this approach will not provide an optimal Internet performance and lacks the advantages of a true end-to-end connectivity, including meaningful access statistics for your web services. So offering your Internet content and all your connection points over IPv6 offers clear advantages. The Internet grew from approximately 360 million users in 2000 to more than 2 billion in 2011.[*] The growth rate in 2010 was approximately 300 million users.

---

[*] www.internetworldstats.com/stats.htm (*http://www.internetworldstats.com/stats.htm*)

IPv6 is running on your network now

Many people do not understand that IPv6 is enabled on all new business and home computers sold in the last few years. Microsoft Windows Vista, Windows 7, Windows Server 2008, MAC OS X, Linux, Android, AIX, HP-UX, and others are generating IPv6 traffic on corporate and home network segments around the world. Some operating system implementations of IPv6 include the installation and automatic activation of transition mechanisms such as tunneling or translation. There are two potential unintended consequences if these are not managed properly: poor application performance associated with unneeded DNS entries, and potential security risks.

The first two items in this list (lack of IPv4 addresses, and customer or corporate demand) are not really predictable, so your best option is to prepare for IPv6 anyway so you will be ready when the time comes. Before you can actually deploy IPv6, you need to allow for a long planning phase, so my recommendation is to get that done as soon as possible. During planning, you will get a good picture of what's required for the different parts of your network, so you can define milestones and timelines for deployment. The moment when you really need IPv6 might be different for different parts of your network, so it's important to have a clear picture of what integration involves. You can easily resolve the risks associated with the fourth item (IPv6 currently running on your network) if you understand how IPv6 works and can make a few simple configuration adjustments.

Opportunities of IPv6 Integration

Just as we can choose to label half a glass of water "half full" or "half empty," we can choose to complain about the IPv6 features we don't like, or focus on the opportunities and master the challenges IPv6 presents. There are quite a few opportunities, so let's identify them.

When you ask people who manage IPv4 networks, "what would you change in your network design if you could start all over with all the operational experience you have today?" you get very interesting answers. Most people have a whole list of things that haven't proven to be so clever over the years, and they have many ideas for how they could improve their addressing plan or other network designs.

This is the opportunity that IPv6 offers. With many years of experience running IP networks, we now have the chance to design our future IP network with IPv6 and its advanced features. To seize this opportunity, we must take all our operational experience, include it in our new concepts, and add the possibilities that the new and extended features of IPv6 offer. You can achieve this only if you plan ahead while there is time, and even more importantly, only if everyone involved in the planning has been given a thorough education and the opportunity to play with IPv6 in the lab to understand its implications.

Specifically, you have the opportunity to create new concepts and designs for the following:

- Addressing
- Network and routing
- Network management
- Security

The importance of this opportunity can be expressed in cost. If you create useful designs, you improve performance and make network maintenance, administration, and troubleshooting much easier and less expensive. Useful designs save yearly returning operational cost. For example, if you consider security when creating an address design, you can optimize the address format for optimal performance in processing ACLs (access control lists) in security devices. When your designs have clear rules, they are easier to enforce and make management and troubleshooting more efficient.

How to Save Money when Integrating IPv6

When you're working on a high-level implementation plan (discussed in Chapter 2) and determining the order of the steps to complete, it's important to consider what other IT projects are planned for the next three to five years.

When I ask customers this question, I often get answers such as:

- We will move our data center in 12 months.
- We will redesign our DMZ in two years.
- We will evaluate new core routers next year and plan deployment for the year after.
- We will have to replace our mainframes in 2013.
- We will migrate our clients to Windows 7 next year.
- We will introduce VoIP next year.
- We plan to use cloud services.
- We will outsource our backbone (or other services).

If you run all these projects without considering IPv6, you're wasting a lot of money. If you move your data center without accounting for IPv6, you will probably touch it all again soon after. If you evaluate new core routers without clear requirements for IPv6 support, you may choose a model that will not support your IPv6 integration optimally. Because a router is a high-end IPv4-optimized router and costs a lot of money doesn't mean it is also a high-end IPv6 router with all the features you need. Asking for IPv6 support for a core router is not sufficient; you have to be much more specific about what features are required to support your transition plan. And to be able to be more specific, you need a high-level implementation plan. The same is true for security devices such as firewalls or intrusion-detection systems. Most customers' core router environment has a life cycle of more than five years. If you buy new core routers next year, chances are really low that you won't have to enable IPv6 during their lifetime.

If you redesign your DMZ without understanding how you will design security for a dual-stack network, you may find later that you would have done it differently had you known about the requirements for IPv6. So, again, you can save money if you consider IPv6 right from the beginning. The same rule goes for all other possible projects on this list, such as introducing Windows 7, Windows Server 2008, or any other service.

When it comes to introducing a completely new service, such as VoIP, you must ask another important question: is it possible to integrate this new service as IPv6-only right from the beginning? If the answer is yes—and it could be, in the example of VoIP—this has several advantages. One is that if you go the IPv6-only route right from the beginning, you don't have to touch it again in this regard. It runs on the future technology. Why spend time on testing and implementing it with IPv4 if you can afford to go IPv6-only right away? The other advantage is that it may free up or save IPv4 addresses that you might need for other purposes or in the event that you run out of your internal IPv4 address space.

Your opportunity to save money with your IPv6 integration lies in aligning it with other IT projects, with your regular product life cycles and in considering IPv6 in all your vendor and product evaluations and vendor and supplier contracts. So turn on IPv6 in your head, and whatever you do in your network from this point forward, do it with IPv6 integration in mind.

When You Outsource

I have one very important recommendation with respect to outsourcing contracts. If you sign an outsourcing contract that will run for 5 or even 10 years, you'd better make sure to address the IPv6 support question. Having your high-level implementation plan worked out already will be an important part of requesting the specific IPv6 support you need and will help you define the right SLAs (service-level agreements) for IPv6.

Companies that outsource everything tend to think that they don't need to care because it's their supplier's job. But you may want to make sure that the supplier is aware of the situation and has a roadmap that meets your needs. He needs to understand the requirements coming from the public space with IPv6-only users on the Internet. He should also be able to provide your public services as dual-stack services with a good IPv4 and IPv6 performance, and also be aware of the requirements for any applications you might introduce that need IPv6 support in the internal network. Failing to do so can severely limit your services or create high-cost and high-risk transitions. And for sure, if you want to add IPv6 services during the lifetime of the contract, it'll cost a lot more than if you include it right from the beginning.

Summary

We can summarize this chapter with these three facts:

- IPv6 is inevitable.
- We don't know exactly when time pressure comes for us.
- It will take us several years to deploy IPv6 in all our networks.

The best strategy you can choose is to plan early, start walking the walk toward your future network, and plan for a meaningful roadmap and milestones that align with other projects and product lifecycles—and do it all while you're not under any time pressure. To get started, read on to Chapter 2, which covers strategy and planning. Remember, every long journey starts with the first step.

Quote

As a lead-in to Chapter 2 about planning, I offer this quote from Fred Wettling, Bechtel Fellow, who is the sponsor for IPv6 deployment within the Bechtel Corporation. Bechtel is one of the earliest global enterprises to implement IPv6, with its initiative starting in 2005.

> Prudent organizations will constantly assess and adapt to changes in technology. On a macro level, we are seeing key trends that will be enabled by or impact the use of technology. These trends include urbanization and demographic changes, new patterns of mobility, new consumption patterns, increased levels of individualizations, a more knowledge-based economy, the digital lifestyle, convergence of technologies, and ubiquitous intelligence. IBM's "Smarter Planet" concept describes a world that is more instrumented, interconnected and intelligent.
>
> The ability to connect people, information, and services on a unified basis has been made possible through the Internet as seen in the flood of new Internet-based products and services in the last two decades. IPv6 is an important part of the continued growth of the Internet in many perspectives. First, the increasing number of things connected to the Internet is exceeding the available IPv4 addresses. The Internet of Things is becoming a reality. Second, new products and services are enabled by technologies that use IPv6 or require IPv6 support. Third, IPv6 is already enabled or running in any organization that has purchased a new computer or mobile device with a current operating system within the last couple of years. Finally, in the near future, some people, information, and services will only be available by using IPv6.
>
> IPv6 technology in commercial products and services are much better than they were a few years ago, but many still do not have the needed IPv6 support. From this perspective, any IPv6 implementation may be directly or indirectly influenced by others. Awareness of this constraint in important in IPv6 planning, but should not hamper the start of work where IPv6 functions are working properly. Each organization should assess the inevitable need to manage IPv6-enabled devices and services for its internal operation and connection with others. The IPv6 implementation will take time, and it's not too early to start now.

CHAPTER 2

Planning for IPv6

This chapter is all about planning for IPv6. It outlines methodologies and procedures, describes the steps and stages of the planning process, and discusses different areas such as routing, security, and central services like DNS and IP address management.

People often ask for best practices. But for IPv6, there aren't really any best practices yet because we don't have years of operational experience from which we can say that something has proven to work well. So we need to draw from our operational experience with IPv4 networks and apply what we have learned about IPv6 so far.

The more time we have for planning and testing, the more likely it is that we can deploy IPv6 in digestible steps and the better we can learn from and adapt with each step. This is the main reason to start as early as possible.

Business Relevance

Part of your IPv6 planning should be to identify any business relevance for IPv6 deployment. Business relevance may include products or services that communicate over a network and are sold commercially or used for business operations. Google, Facebook, and many other companies have chosen to expose their content over both IPv4 and IPv6, ensuring that customers can reach them regardless of the Internet protocol version the customer uses. Products from Sony PlayStation to Panasonic Internet pet cams to Canon network printers to most current cell phones support IPv6.

What Are You Talking About?

I notice that in many discussions of IPv6 integration, there is no differentiation between the areas of deployment. Different parts of your network have different requirements and timelines, so it helps a lot to break the discussion down and look at each of them separately. Very often, people seem to disagree, but when you analyze the discussion you find that both parties are right; they just don't realize that they're talking about different things.

We know from Chapter 1 that the reasons for introducing IPv6 in your internal network are different from the reasons for introducing it in your public-facing services. The world does not really care how you access your internal servers, databases, and services. The world cares about how you can be reached, and likewise you should care about how you can reach the world.

You may separate your planning into the following areas:

- Core/Backbone
- User/Customer networks
- Data center
- DMZ/Internet (customer facing)

The requirements and challenges for IPv6 may be different for each of these areas. So, for instance, you may have enough IPv4 addresses for your internal network and your services, but you want to make sure that your Internet connectivity isn't limited in any way. In this case, you decide to make your DMZ dual-stacked as soon as possible, while you have enough time left, to integrate IPv6 in your internal network.

But then if you plan a data center move for next year, this will probably be the impetus for deploying IPv6 in that part of your network—not because you face time pressure, but because it will save you a lot of extra cost for a later migration, which would eventually be due anyway. Or you may want to prepare your internal network for the unpredictable case that new applications and services require IPv6 features or the extended address space, or that the demand for secure mobility can be best met with IPv6. Deploying IPv6 in your internal network may be a major task that takes three or more years in larger environments. Because you know that IPv6 is inevitable and to prepare for the aforementioned situations, it's better to start planning today.

 Generally, you can say that all the money you invest in IPv6 is an investment in future technology, while all investments in IPv4 are an investment in an end-of-life technology.

In many cases, integrating IPv6 for public-facing services is the first step, and it is also considered a good approach because it is one of the easier parts of integration. Starting where it is easier allows you to use that part of the project to gather experience and better prepares you to tackle the internal network with its higher complexity.

There are several methods to deploy IPv6, and they are discussed in the following sections. In reality, you might choose an approach that combines elements of each model, but the models give useful guidelines for the order of the steps and activities you'll complete during your journey.

Core to Edge

Core to edge is the approach you will probably choose if you have the time. It has several advantages. In this approach, you start deploying IPv6 where it is easiest. The equipment you use in the core has the longest history of implementation and deployment, so the IPv6 stacks are more mature and you can usually deploy with the least upgrade effort. The complexity of IPv6 integration increases when you move to the edge. Stacks are less mature, implementations are either not available or are in an early, buggy stage, and application compatibility and interoperability can be an issue. Vendor support may be in its early stages too. So while you work on the core, you'll build all your experience; and by the time you get to the edge, hopefully the market has matured and you've had the time to resolve the edge issues in your labs.

Another important advantage of this approach is that while you work on deployment in the core, your critical user or customer traffic still flows over the IPv4 infrastructure, so you can deploy IPv6 with no risk or pressure. You can also implement management and security, and then test everything carefully before you allow user and customer traffic. This approach helps you train your people, get experience in managing the new infrastructure, and build your support teams, such as help desk and second-level support.

Edge to Core

Edge to core is the approach to choose when you need to roll out IPv6 to customers or clients quickly. This may be the case when you run out of IPv4 addresses and can't cover the demand for growth anymore, when a new service requires a lot more addresses than you have or when a new application is needed, that requires IPv6.

The project risks rise significantly when you choose this approach, so you may want to avoid this situation by planning while there is time. Besides the fact that urgency is always a critical factor when you're introducing new technologies, the risks and costs are high because you're starting where the complexity is highest, you'll face project delays due to interoperability issues and unexpected bugs, and—most importantly— you'll have to enable user and customer traffic over your infrastructure before you've had the time to carefully build and test it. Your engineers and support organization will have to manage the infrastructure even though they haven't had time to develop the experience necessary to support it efficiently. Service outages are much more likely to happen with this approach.

IPv6 Islands

IPv6 islands are the approach you can use when you must deploy IPv6 to specific applications, customers, or parts of the network as a first step. Tunnels may be used to carry IPv6 traffic over IPv4 subnets to interconnect the IPv6 islands.

Economic considerations may be one of the main reasons to choose this approach. It also reduces the project scope for deployment and the number of systems that have to be changed. It allows you to deploy IPv6 where it is most needed first. So, for instance, if you choose to upgrade your DMZ first in order to be publicly reachable over IPv6, you're using an island approach. Or if you choose to deploy a new service as IPv6-only right from the beginning, this would be another island approach. Islands can also be used for trials to have a controlled environment and limit the impact and the risks.

Organizations that use external services, such as web hosting, can work with the service provider to enable IPv6. This method takes advantage of any IPv6 implementation experience the service provider may already have.

You must carefully evaluate whether the island approach makes sense at large scale. You have to weigh the advantages against the complexity of managing a heterogenous network, which always increases operational cost and carries a higher risk of misconfiguration and errors.

Planning and Deployment Methodologies

All roads lead to Rome. You probably have a well-established framework and procedure to run your technology projects. Introducing IPv6 works like almost any other technology project. If you do a perfect job, your users and customers will not even notice that they are using a new transport protocol (most users don't care anyway—they may not even know what a protocol is).

In a large network, IPv6 can only be integrated with a phased approach and a gradual transition (integration). In this section, I'll outline common approaches that have been used by different organizations for IPv6 deployment and have proven to work well.

How to Get Started

Every long journey starts with a first step; after that, things become much clearer. But what is the first step to planning for IPv6? The complexity of an IPv6 project comes from the fact that we are adding a transport layer protocol, which means that all networking components are affected. It also means that all networking and application teams and IT groups have to collaborate to make the integration work.

To get started, you need an idea of where you want to go. This is the objective of a high-level design. Before you can actually define your goal, you need to take the preparatory steps outlined in the following sections.

Use existing change processes

Most organizations have an existing process in place to introduce application and infrastructure changes. This process often includes a progression from a development environment through some type of quality assurance (QA) stage and finally into production. IPv6 deployments should leverage existing change controls. The current processes may have to be adjusted to account for IPv6 features. With regard to IPv6 it is important to ensure the coordination across all teams. Further, existing development and QA environments should be configured to support end-to-end IPv6 communications to ensure that, going forward, all products and services deployed in production have been verified to operate in a dual-stack environment.

Network health and reality check

The introduction of IPv6 can be successful only if it is integrated in a healthy and well-performing network. So, before you even start the planning phase, you may want to use the opportunity to do some house cleaning. This involves checking the health of all components, routing efficiency and stability, configurations, addressing plan structure, and many more. It is vital to have a good understanding of traffic flows, rerouting in case of failures, and application performance, and to verify the functionality of core services such as DNS, DHCP, firewalls, and intrusion detection systems.

At the same time, you can perform a reality check. We often find that the real situation in the network differs from the concepts behind it, even in the most professional environments. A reality check verifies that the real-world network behavior conforms to your design and documented implementation. This check is essential because it lays the foundation for the planning phase.

In reality, the optimization of the current environment can also be an outcome of the IPv6 project. But before you base your new address design or security concept on the current concept, you want to ensure the current concept conforms to reality.

Create an IPv6 Governance and Project Team

For a successful project, you must develop a well-structured IPv6 integration project team. Because IPv6 integration touches every component and department in your IT environment, everybody has to be involved, including key business stakeholders. Managing this task in a large organization can be a challenge. A good approach to coordinate all activities efficiently is to have one or two people lead the project as IPv6 program managers. The program managers organize all activities with the project leaders of each individual group (such as security, routing, applications, etc).

Education and Consulting

For the design of a high-level implementation plan every department that deals with the network and its services must be included. Before the team can start discussing a high-level implementation plan, however, all the team members must be thoroughly trained and understand both the obvious and the more subtle differences between IPv6 and IPv4. In the initial phase, this training includes executives, architects, planners, the security and routing team, server and client teams, and application groups—all the groups that should also be included in the planning and design. The team needs a good and thorough understanding of the entire IPv6 protocol and all its new features and possibilities. In this first phase, it is also very important to launch awareness campaigns at the top executive level and include all stakeholders.

Simply applying your IPv4 concepts to the IPv6 network will carry over IPv4's limitations to your IPv6 network. By building an IPv6 network, you have the opportunity to build a next-generation network that is capable of supporting the applications and services of the future. Without a thorough understanding of the new features, you waste this opportunity.

In a later stage of the project, all groups will need more in-depth training and the possibility to build and run labs to get a feeling for the protocol and create more refined concepts for each area of the network. In this stage, you also need to include other groups such as support staff, help desk, customer contact groups, and sales and marketing people. The list of groups to be trained at this stage may vary depending on the business and the type of organization.

If your organization develops applications for internal use or for the market, make sure you train the developers in IPv6 with a specific focus on developing IP-version-agnostic applications that behave well in both IPv4 and IPv6 networks, but also in dual-stacked networks.

A note on consulting: there are various degrees of engagement with consultants. You can try to do the entire integration with your own resources, or you can choose to fully outsource the project. I do not recommend trying to do it all with internal resources. While you create new concepts for all the parts of your network, it is a good idea to get external perspectives to broaden the scope as much as possible. This is your opportunity to redesign your network, so at least get second opinions before you deploy. At the same time, it is important to involve all your teams in the design phase, because they are familiar with the internal procedures and policies and they are the ones who will have to operate the network. So a combined approach is usually the most efficient for everyone. With this approach, your staff can learn and profit from external perspectives and experience, and will not have to reinvent the wheel. Bringing in experienced consultants to work with your teams can be considered (and budgeted as) on-the-job education.

High-Level Concept

The biggest and most costly mistake is to assume that IPv6 is not that different from IPv4 after all, and that with all your IPv4 experience, it will be pretty easy to create concepts for IPv6. While that approach may work at first glance, it means you squander all the options and possibilities the new protocol offers. For instance, if you create an address plan with the limited cell-engrained mindset you've developed from 15 years of operating IPv4 networks—where the highest priority has always been to preserve address space—it's a safe bet that the address concept will be like a straitjacket for the future and that in five years you'll be saying, "if only I could start all over again..." Creating concepts like this is way more expensive than giving IPv6 enough attention right from the beginning.

One important ingredient of the high-level design is going through all the designs that exist in your environment right now, reevaluating them, and asking yourself what components have stood the test of time and what you would do differently if you could start over. Take what you've learned from operating an IPv4 network and integrate it into your IPv6 concept (obviously, don't copy whatever you did to conserve address space), combining it with the new features and possibilities IPv6 offers.

The high-level concept answers the questions: what is our long-term goal—where do we want to be in 5–10 years? What will our network look like, what will our services probably be like, should we plan for going IPv6-only as soon as possible (and if yes, in what areas of the network?), or should we plan for a long-term dual-stack strategy? Do we have enough IPv4 addresses to go dual-stack long term? What will our security and routing designs look like? How do we manage the coexistence of IPv4 with IPv6 and a dual-stacked network?

In many cases, the network will predominantly be IPv4 for a long time, with growing elements of IPv6. At some point in the future, it may be a mainly dual-stacked network with decreasing IPv4 support while slowly moving toward a predominantly IPv6 network. Over these different periods, you may use different mechanisms to support it. Even for many years to come, we may have to support some single IPv4-only applications. In the early days of deployment, we support them by running dual-stack if possible, but in the future we may choose to turn off IPv4 in the network and find other mechanisms to support these IPv4 applications.

As part of the high-level design, you will create an IPv6 address plan, a routing and a security design. At this point, you need to involve upper management, if you haven't already done so, although it's usually not yet possible to know how much IPv6 deployment will cost. You can answer the cost question only after you've assessed the network based on the IPv6 requirements outlined in the upcoming section, "Network Assessment."

Mind the Apps

Most applications simply rely on the host operating system for network operations and services for handling IPv4 or IPv6 traffic. However, some applications may exhibit different or undesirable behavior when end-to-end IPv6 is enabled. Key things to look for are applications that log the IP addresses of network traffic or include control/configuration files containing IP addresses instead of a URL and DNS for name-address resolution. Particularly, any applications that make direct calls to the IP layer will probably have to be adjusted to work well in a dual-stack world.

Ways to Get There

Once you know where you want to go, the next step is to determine how you want to get there, where you want to start, and what the important intermediary steps are on the way to your final goal which, in the long term, should be an IPv6-only network. In other words, you define your roadmap for step-by-step deployment.

When answering these questions, it's important that you:

- Align your roadmap with your overall IT strategy and other IT projects that have been defined for the coming three to five years. As pointed out in the section "How to Save Money when Integrating IPv6" on page 10, in Chapter 1, aligning the deployment of IPv6 with other ongoing projects can save a lot of money.
- Align the deployment timeline with life cycles of products in your network, such as core routers, firewalls and applications.

There is no one-size-fits-all strategy, too diverse are the individual environments and requirements. I know from experience that once you lay out everything you know about your current environment, your final goal, and your requirements for IPv6, other IT projects, and product life cycles, suddenly a sensible path emerges that makes best use of your resources and options while minimizing costs and risks.

Once you have an overall plan of your journey and the milestones to hit along the way, you will define subprojects. An incremental approach is essential to reducing risks. For each milestone, you will create detailed implementation plans with more specific requirements. You should then verify each milestone for conformance and test it thoroughly before moving on to the next project step.

Define IPv6 Requirements

Based on your high-level implementation plan, you can start to define IPv6 requirements for all the devices, operating systems, and applications in your network. The requirements have to be very specific (you won't get around quoting RFC numbers) and will vary depending on the device. It is not specific enough to require an IPv6 function—in some cases, you will also have to specify suboptions or message types.

For example, DHCPv6 supports many options (you can find all the options in the DHC working group at *http://datatracker.ietf.org/wg/dhc*), but you may not need all of them for your purposes. Or if you require your new firewall to be able to filter on extension headers, you may want to list specific headers, such as the routing header type 2 defined for Mobile IPv6. You also want to make sure your firewall doesn't pass packets with illegal extension headers, deals accurately with the deprecated routing header type 0, and inspects the content of tunneled packets.

The requirements specification serves four purposes:

- It is a reference for the IPv6 functions required on each interface in the network.
- It is a guideline for the system assessment.
- It is a guideline for software and hardware vendors to assess the functionality of current versions and verify roadmaps for future purchases. It is the base for vendor RFIs.
- It is a foundation for conformance and acceptance testing.

Network Assessment

Now that you have your IPv6 requirements specification, you can start assessing all your network devices and services. This assessment is used to categorize all the devices, operating systems, and products for their level of IPv6 capability.

The assessment must cover the following:

- Hardware
- Operating systems, versions, and patch levels
- Applications, versions, and patch levels

All items can then be categorized as follows:

- Systems that comply with IPv6 requirements
- Systems that must be upgraded to comply with IPv6 requirements (the upgrade can be software or hardware or both)
- Systems that must be replaced to comply with IPv6 requirements

 If you have a *CMDB* (configuration management database) or are in the process of building one, this is a good opportunity to populate it or to start building it, if you haven't already.

This assessment clarifies the scope of your IPv6 deployment project. You may find that you need to adjust the roadmap that you created in your high-level design. And now you can estimate costs for each step in your roadmap, because the assessment has helped you identify what investments and how much effort will be necessary for the deployment. Some of your findings may also have an impact on integration mechanisms you've chosen; for instance, you may find that a service that you assumed could be upgraded to work in a dual-stacked environment has to be replaced but has no alternative available.

In general, IPv6 compatibility in your applications probably has a bigger impact on your integration plan than equipment support. And the more custom-developed or highly customized in-house applications you use, the higher the chance they won't work with IPv6 and may not even be upgradable. So make sure you allow for enough time in the planning and testing stages to find solutions to these challenges.

Evaluate Vendors, Products, and Service Providers

This is a perfect time to reassess your vendor portfolio. Whether a device, service, or application has the required IPv6 support may not be the only criterion. You may want to find out what your vendor's roadmap looks like to determine whether he will be up to date in following development and offering state-of-the-art products. Obviously, the importance of this step varies for different devices and products. Specifically, for core network devices and services that usually have a long life cycle—such as core routers, firewalls, management and monitoring tools, and DDI (DNS, DHCP & IPAM) solutions—it is crucial to have a vendor who guarantees high performance products, professional support and a good future development roadmap.

When it comes to your ISP, it is not sufficient to ask for basic IPv6 connectivity. You want to know what kind of connectivity you will get; whether it will be tunneled or native has an impact on performance and scalability. You also want to know what the ISP's peering connections to the IPv6 Internet are.

Build Labs and Pilots

Labs are probably your most important playground on your way to becoming an IPv6 expert and reducing deployment risks. The lab serves many different purposes. First and foremost, it's a place for experimenting, learning, and gathering experience, and then you take that knowledge back to the planning process to be integrated in deployment concepts. You may have several options in your high-level strategy—such as the choice of a routing protocol, different solutions or designs, or various vendors and products—where you need to evaluate which selection best suits your requirements or performs better in a given environment, and to test compatibility of different products. You should always evaluate and test your design choices and deployment steps in a lab before finalizing the deployment plan to reduce risks and project delays.

The ideal scenario is having a completely separate lab that mirrors your production environment as closely as possible. You use the lab to test your deployment strategy, fix bugs, and learn how to troubleshoot IPv6. It is also the perfect playground to train your support staff for operating an IPv6 network. You can use it to document your deployment plan, implementation, and configuration, and to create functional specifications. Finally, you can perform quality assurance and conformance tests in the lab.

During the different stages of deployment, the lab will probably change. So, if you choose a core to edge approach, you will first want to test all backbone functionality including addressing, routing, and security and how the components interact. Next, you'll test network services such as address management, DNS design, and behavior in combination with services and applications and so on. You probably also want to do performance and load tests for your chosen scenarios to find out ahead of time if your network can deal with the additional traffic and the mechanisms that you have chosen, and to determine whether core systems (routers, switches, firewalls, and other security devices) perform under load. Every step you test may deliver findings that make you refine your deployment plan.

 IPv6 will not double your traffic. You have to consider that you are gradually moving traffic from IPv4 transport to IPv6 transport. So, generally, more IPv6 traffic means less IPv4 traffic. But there are still things to consider and test—for instance, if you run dual-stack, in the future your switches will not only deal with IPv4 broadcast traffic, but also with IPv6 multicast traffic.

Once you have evaluated your vendor candidates, you'll need to use the lab to test their products for conformance to the project's standards and requirements and to find possible bugs. You have to be prepared for the fact that many IPv6 implementations are early versions, and therefore may be immature and have more bugs in the beginning than you are used to from their current IPv4 counterparts. Allow enough time in the lab to test this, because it may save you a lot of headaches during later stages of the project. Finding unexpected bugs usually delays projects, as it requires you to solve the issues with the vendor and wait for patches before you can move on. In general, whatever you test in your lab—be it verification of concepts, stacks, devices, or applications—the earlier you find any issues, incompatibilities, and bugs, the easier and less expensive it is to find new solutions or fix code.

Refine Your High-Level Strategy and Define Low-Level Deployment Plans

Once you have verified your high-level strategy, know the state of your IPv6 readiness, and have tested all your options and vendor products, you can refine your high-level concept and develop detailed, low-level deployment plans for each specific network and service area. You should place these plans on a meaningful timeline and account for all interdependencies.

At this point, you will also perform a risk assessment and develop a risk-mitigation strategy. The results of this assessment may affect your integration and security strategy, and they also provide the foundation for a fallback plan.

Each low-level implementation plan will have detailed descriptions of implementation procedures (including setups and configurations for all components or applications), schedules and timelines, backout plans, acceptance criteria, and tests to be performed. Before you implement IPv6 in production, you will probably want to thoroughly test the implementation plan in your lab.

In the long term, for the operational phase of a dual-stack network, you will need to ensure that all management and change processes are fully synchronized so you can keep the same level of functionality and security for both protocols. Changing configurations should be a single coordinated process for both protocols.

The Golden Rule Set

Here's a summary of the golden rules of IPv6 integration:

- If you haven't deployed IPv6 yet, make sure to block all IPv6 traffic coming from and going to the Internet (native and tunneled).
- Add IPv6 requirements to all purchasing policies and outsourcing contracts.
- Before investing in extending or fixing your IPv4 infrastructure, evaluate IPv6.
- Go native IPv6 wherever you can and go IPv6-only wherever you can.
- Minimize the use of transition mechanisms.
- Avoid translation mechanisms wherever possible.
- Turn off transition mechanisms as soon as they are no longer needed.
- Don't wait for a flag day or killer application.
- Use the natural life cycles of your devices, operating systems, and applications.
- Align the integration of IPv6 with other IT projects.
- Use the opportunities IPv6 offers and take the chance to redesign your network for the future.
- Go for step-by-step integration and learn as you go—this is the most cost-effective and least risky strategy.
- Be careful when dealing with Asia! The Internet growth rate in Asia is much higher than in other parts of the world, so many Asian countries are much more advanced with IPv6. If you have business partners or make acquisitions in Asia, you may be faced with integrating and communicating with IPv6 networks sooner rather than later. If Asia is your market for selling IP-based services or products, IPv6 support is most probably a minimum requirement.
- Watch your public services, and deploy IPv6 to be reachable and connected from and to the whole Internet.

To broaden your perspective on planning considerations for IPv6, refer to the book *Global IPv6 Strategies: From Business Analysis to Operational Planning* by Patrick Grossetete, Ciprian P. Popoviciu, and Fred Wettling (Cisco Press). It is the definitive guide to IPv6 decision making for nontechnical business leaders and contains many detailed case studies of organizations in different sectors.

Choices and Designs

While creating all these new designs, you have many choices to make. Take the time to analyze and understand the new features of IPv6, because only then can you unlock its potential. If you simply try to mirror your IPv4 designs to the IPv6 world, you miss the opportunity to create networks that will not only be ready to support similar network services, but which will also scale to support future applications and services. Remember that IPv6 represents a unique opportunity to create an environment that sustains innovation and facilitates competitive differentiation.

Routing and Routing Protocols

With IPv6's extended address space, having a good address design is more important than with IPv4. The address length offers new options for a hierarchical addressing structure, which in the future might be more based on geographical aspects at the upper levels to support efficient aggregation.

In general, routing and forwarding principles are no different in an IPv6 network. We have some features to optimize forwarding efficiency, such as a fixed-length IPv6 header, extension headers (which are inserted only if options are needed), and the fact that IPv6 routers do not fragment anymore. We can use the flow label to optimize data flows.

It's important to understand that in the early days of the IPv6 Internet, forwarding will probably not be much faster, because most of the traffic is still being tunneled over IPv4 paths and there aren't too many IPv6 backbones available yet. Once more than 50% of the Internet backbones are native IPv6, we will start to experience the IPv6 forwarding speeds.

The original plan for IPv6 was to not allocate *provider-independent* (PI) addresses at all. An early design goal for IPv6 was to not only solve the address situation, but also the problem with overflowing Internet routing tables. Just like with IPv4, the IANA distributes the IPv6 address space to the *RIRs* (regional Internet registries), but mainly based on geography in order to keep the root routing tables as small as possible. It turned out that the zero PI space wasn't a sustainable policy in the real world. So we are back to having PI space, which partially breaks the hierarchical model based on geography and thereby creates more entries in global routing tables. An example: PI space means that a company headquartered in Switzerland with a global network may get PI address space from RIPE, the RIR for Europe. For the US locations of that company, the US-based ISPs will have to announce the route to this RIPE prefix.

Also, in the future IPv6 routing tables will not contain 32-bit address entries, but rather 128-bit address entries. And during the transition time in dual-stack networks, routers will maintain two routing tables, one for IPv4 and one for IPv6. The vendors will have to make sure that forwarding is efficient, done in hardware, and that the routers use resources efficiently so the routing tables take up the minimum possible memory.

There are two different types of routing protocols. An *IGP* (interior gateway protocol) is used within an *AS* (autonomous system), which represents an administrative domain. Different autonomous systems are connected through *EGPs* (exterior gateway protocols).

IGPs

There are two types of IGPs. Some IGPs use a *distance-vector algorithm* to make routing decisions. In this case, a router knows only about his neighbors and has no picture of the whole network. *Link-state protocols*, on the other hand, have maps of the whole network and make all routing information available to every router in the AS.

For IPv6 networks, the following IGPs are available:

RIPng (RFC 2080)

> RIP is a distance-vector protocol that uses the Bellman-Ford algorithm.[*] It is easy to use but is far less efficient than OSPF and IS-IS, described next. It has all the limitations that RIPv4 always had: its diameter is limited, routing loops can create long convergence times, and the metrics don't represent line speeds because they are based on hop counts. It is not a recommended routing protocol for enterprise networks.

OSPFv3 (RFC 5340)

> OSPFv3 is a link-state-based protocol that uses Dijkstra's algorithm[†] to calculate a tree of shortest paths (SPF). OSPFv3 uses link-local addresses to exchange routing information (which is very helpful in the case of renumbering) and eliminates OSPFv2 authentication, because it now uses standard IPv6 authentication. As defined in RFC 5340, OSPFv3 runs as a separate process. You still need OSPFv2 to manage your IPv4 network, and each version maintains separate routing tables. RFC 5838 defines extensions that support multiple address families in OSPFv3. This protocol extension is in the early stages, so vendor support is currently limited, if available at all. Ask for the vendor's roadmap.

---

[*] *http://en.wikipedia.org/wiki/Bellman%E2%80%93Ford_algorithm*

[†] *http://en.wikipedia.org/wiki/Dijkstra%27s_algorithm*

IS-IS (RFC 5308)

IS (Intermediate System) is the OSI (Open Systems Interconnection) term for router. IS-IS is a link-state protocol and also uses Dijkstra's algorithm. It is an ISO (International Organization for Standardization) protocol and does not rely on IP to exchange routing information. It is similar to OSPF, but is considered to be easier to configure and manage by many administrators. IPv6 is fully integrated, and does not run as a separate process as in the current OSPFv3 versions. For many years, it was mainly used in provider networks and wasn't very common in the United States. In recent years, however, it has become more common and is being used more and more in the enterprise space.

EIGRP for IPv6

EIGRP was developed by Cisco Systems. It is a hybrid protocol, taking the best of both the distance-vector and link-state-based worlds, and is based on DUAL (diffusing update algorithm).‡ It runs as a separate process, so to manage IPv4 and IPv6, two instances must be used. For larger environments, I usually recommend using OSPF or IS-IS instead. In a hub-spoke topology though, EIGRP performs really well. Besides generally being less scalable than OSPFv3 and IS-IS, EIGRPv6 is supported only on Cisco gear, which creates a vendor lock-in and can also cause delays when you need updates, which are often faster in a competitive multivendor-supported standard.

For your dual-stack network of the future, your choices are probably OSPFv2 and OSPFv3 (or in the future possibly OSPF with multi-address family support) versus IS-IS. RIPng doesn't scale in enterprise networks, and EIGRP is a proprietary solution that comes with a vendor lock-in and doesn't scale as well as OSPFv3 and IS-IS.

There are probably not any real technically based pros or cons for OSPF versus IS-IS. Some companies run both OSPF versions and have no issues with that method, while others prefer to migrate their OSPFv2 to IS-IS in order to have one single instance in the future. IS-IS will likely become even more common in the future. Your decision between the two protocols will be influenced more by other factors, such as building know-how if you've been using OSPF and want to start integrating IS-IS. If you choose OSPFv3, you'll still have to learn some things, but the difference from OSPFv2 is not as significant. Your choice also depends on corporate culture and market factors such as available skills and resources on the market.

 While the difference in managing OSPFv2 versus managing OSPFv3 is not so significant for the administrator, be aware that there are more subtle differences in the structure of OSPFv3 that are significant from a design perspective.

‡ *http://en.wikipedia.org/wiki/Diffusing_update_algorithm*

EGPs

The Border Gateway Protocol (BGP) is the core routing protocol in the Internet and is used to exchange routing information between autonomous systems. There is no actual BGP for IPv6, but there are IPv6 extensions to BGP-4, based on the defined BGP-4 multiprotocol extensions. It can also be used in very large enterprise networks where OSPF doesn't scale well anymore.

Address Plan

The address plan is a challenge for most. We have all been well trained to conserve addresses, and the training has been so efficient that this rule is stored in our brain and body cells. We have to overcome this reflex action before we can create a useful IPv6 address concept for 128-bit addresses. So what are the rules, how can address concepts be designed for IPv6?

Before we start, though, let's go over something that may help you to slowly overcome your address-conservation reflex and free your mind from its limited thinking. Use this as your daily mantra while you work on an address concept.

Consider the numbers of IPv6 address allocation. By January 2011, approximately 145,000 /32s have been allocated[§]. In 2010, 5,800 /32s were given out, and in 2009 the number was 1,000 /32s. Now note that one single /32 provides more subnets than the entire IPv4 address space provides addresses. This is because the IPv4 address has 32 bits for the whole address, including host IDs, while a /32 provides 32 prefix bits and each subnet has 64 interface ID bits.

So this means that by 2011, we have allocated 145,000 more IPv6 address space than we ever had with IPv4. Is that a lot? When we calculate how much of the currently defined address space that is, we see it represents a mere 0.027%! And the currently used global space is only a fraction of what we really have—only 2000::/3. With 145,000 /32s, 9.5 billion customers can receive a /48. And each customer can create 65,536 subnets, with each subnet having 64 interface ID bits. Go figure—it will suffice for some years. OK, now shake your cells and read on.

An efficient address plan should group address ranges logically in order to:

- Simplify the configuration and processing of access lists and firewall rules.
- Make addresses easier to recognize by integrating location and/or service and other identifiers in the address.
- Create enough space for extensions (more services) and growth (more locations and users).
- Allow for efficient network management.

§ *http://bgpexpert.com/addrspace-ipv6-2010.php*

This section assumes you are familiar with the technical aspects of the IPv6 address architecture, so I do not cover them here. If you need information, you can find plenty of documents on the Web, or check out Chapter 3 in my companion book, *IPv6 Essentials*, Second Edition (O'Reilly).

What is new?

There are three main differences to consider between IPv4 and IPv6 when you're forming an address plan:

- One of the most obvious differences (besides the length of the address) is that we don't need VLSMs (variable length subnet masks) anymore. The prefix or network part of an IPv6 address is always 64 bits (/64). Even for point-to-point links? Yes, even for point-to-point links (some people choose to change that rule—you will have to decide for yourself). So, in this respect, IPv6 addresses are simpler. No more guessing or misconfiguring of subnet masks. VLSMs have contributed a lot to the complexity of managing IPv4 address space.

- The preceding rule also relates to the following: we no longer have to size subnets to the number of devices in the subnet (in other words, no more address conservation practices necessary). Each and every subnet can potentially have 2^{64} devices. The number of devices for each subnet will be determined by your switch's capacity, so consult your vendor to find out what is possible.

- In IPv6, addresses are assigned to interfaces. So an IPv6 address identifies an interface, not a host. And, in many cases, an interface will be multiaddressed and choose addresses to initiate connections based on policies or default address selection rules.

And please resist the temptation to use larger masks for your subnets such as /96 in order to preserve address space. This will create many problems in the future, as all development is based on the /64 mask. So for instance SLAAC (stateless address autoconfiguration) won't work with non-/64 mask. CGAs (cryptographically generated addresses) are another example of an address that needs the /64 mask because it uses interface ID bits to distribute security keys. And there may be many other processes or services in the future that fail with a non-standard subnet mask. You have enough address space with IPv6! Optimize it for efficient management.

Once you are familiar with the IPv6 address architecture, take the list of things that you would change in your IPv4 address concept if you could start all over, and begin designing your IPv6 address concept. The rules for building a useful address concept have not substantially changed. They are:

- Prefix aggregation
- Subnet consistency
- Use of address types (unique local addresses, ULAs); this one is new to IPv6
- Use of address provisioning and management mechanisms and tools (DHCPv6, SLAAC, IPAM/DDI)
- Security
- Operational aspects such as optimization of filtering rules (performance!)
- Network growth
- Network growth
- Network growth (this is not a typo)

You need to integrate the incredibly large IPv6 address space *in all aspects*. I can't repeat this enough. So, for instance, when it comes to subnet consistency, there is no need to conserve address space anymore.

 For operational ease and to simplify administration, keep all subnets for a certain type of location the same size, regardless of how many users work there. Although this is the best way to go, it may feel uncomfortable in the beginning. The same rule is true if you leave address space free for growth. A good rule to follow is *if your cells don't hurt, your plan isn't quite big enough yet*.

Global addresses versus ULAs

As already mentioned, an IPv6 interface can typically have multiple addresses. Part of your address design is deciding what address types to use. Specifically, you have two options: to generally use global IPv6 addresses, or to use ULAs (unique local addresses) internally. ULAs are defined in RFC 4193, have a prefix of FD00::/8, and are the equivalent of RFC 1918 private addresses in IPv4, which means they are routable but should only be used internally and never routed to the Internet. They can, for instance, be used for an internal deployment or to build a lab when you do not have global IPv6 address space allocated yet.

There is one big difference between the RFC 1918 concept and how these private addresses are used today. Using ULAs does not mean that you need NAT (network address translation) to get outside to the Internet. Because IPv6 interfaces are designed to work with multiple address types, interfaces that need Internet connectivity will simply have a global IPv6 address in addition to the ULA address. When connecting to an internal server, the interface will use its ULA address; and when connecting to the Internet, it will use its global IPv6 address. Don't build NATs for this purpose! RFC 3484 defines default address selection rules to deal with this. So, with this design, internal server systems and databases that should not be reached from outside,will be configured only with ULAs.

> Although with regard to NATs in such a scenario, I have to mention that RFC 6296 defines a stateless network prefix translation (NPTv6) function, designed to provide address independence to the edge network. In the introduction of the RFC, it says that the IETF (Internet Engineering Task Force) does NOT recommend the use of Network Address Translation technology. The technology has mainly be defined to avoid the uncontrolled and private development of incompatible solutions by different vendors. NPTv6 has fewer architectural problems than traditional stateful NAT, as it does a one-to-one address mapping and therefore does not require using ports for a one-to-many address mapping.

When it comes to choosing whether you want to use ULAs or go with global addresses, there are pros and cons to both approaches and many discussions surrounding them. Due to early deployment time, there is not too much operational experience available to draw from. From a technical point of view, you could make either choice—you will have to decide for yourself.

Here are the arguments for ULAs:

- ULAs make you internally independent of your global prefix, which is advantageous if you need to renumber your network. In this case, all your internal systems and communications are not affected. If you have a PI address space, this is not a concern.
- ULAs add a layer of security to your internal infrastructure, as servers and databases with critical data are not reachable from outside. Obviously, you still need firewalls to protect systems, but ULAs offer additional protection.
- Attackers who know some of your global addresses cannot derive the addresses for internal systems.
- ULAs should not be used with NAT, so this is not a concern. Systems that need access to the Internet will get a global IPv6 address in addition to the ULA address.

Now, whether you want to use ULAs is up to you. Many people decide that with the unlimited IPv6 address space, where they can finally address all systems with global addresses, they want to go for this simple option—securing their internal systems with firewalls and having the advantage of administering only one prefix. For those that decide to use both global and ULA, I would hope that IPAM vendors are clever enough to develop systems that can manage multiple prefixes and import the subnet design to the IPAM solution for easy administration. Probably you can choose the same subnetting and interface addressing plan for both prefixes anyway.

Network-level design approaches

The large address space creates opportunities for you to define logical and practical address plans in new and creative ways. As an introductory note, please be aware that it is dangerous to copy too many design aspects from your IPv4 address plan, because chances are good that they are limited designs that make no sense in an IPv6 address plan. That being said, here are some ideas that you can use to get started:

- Redesign and allocate subnets consistently and generously (no conservation thoughts anymore—it must hurt to break this habit!).
- Translate IPv4 subnet IDs into IPv6 subnet IDs.
- Translate IPv4 VLAN IDs into IPv6 subnet IDs.
- Aggregate along geographical boundaries.
- Aggregate along organizational boundaries.
- Assign subnet ranges for data, real-time traffic, security isolation (DMZ), and network functions.
- Assign to identify service types, using specific bits to represent specific service types.

While you ponder your options, don't forget to consider ACLs and how you can design your address plan to optimize their configuration and processing.

Whenever you translate something from your IPv4 address plan to your IPv6 address plan, make sure that you are not also copying *limitations* over to the new concept. You are creating an address concept with a future native IPv6 network in mind, and the dual-stack network is only a transitional state, although it may exist for some years. But once you start running a native IPv6-only network, you'll want the almost unlimited freedom of the address space without having to renumber the network.

For a long time, the recommendation was that ISPs got a /32 from their RIR and organizations, and end sites got a /48 from their provider or a /48 as PI space. RFC 6177 changes the recommended assignment size to end sites. It states that "a one-size-fits-all recommendation of /48 is not nuanced enough for the broad range of end sites and is no longer recommended as a single default." The RFC states that it is in the domain of the operational community to determine the best prefix size for end sites. This introduces some new considerations. When the default prefix was a /48, a change of provider or assignments from different providers always had the same prefix boundary. With the new policy, it is possible that an end site may have to renumber from a larger prefix into a smaller prefix, which means having to collapse subnets. You can prepare for this if you have a /48 and use only the low-order bits first (if the network size allows you to do that). It seems that many providers often assign /56 or /52 prefixes to smaller sites. This rule does not apply to large enterprises; they will always get a /48 or even more. According to RFC 6177, even home users should get more than just a /64 subnet. The development of services in the market suggests that future home networks have multiple subnets (*smart buildings*).

With regard to subnet size, there is nothing in the specification that prevents you from changing the /64 boundary. But I don't recommend that, because doing so will break many other features of IPv6 where applications and processes assume the /64 subnet size. This includes mechanisms such as SLAAC (stateless address autoconfiguration), SEND (secure neighbor discovery), privacy extensions, parts of Mobile IPv6 specifications, PIM-SM (protocol-independent multicast – sparse mode) with embedded-RP, and SHIM6 (site multihoming by IPv6 intermediation), among others. And there may be more developments in the future that assume a /64 boundary. If you change that, all these features will break.

 The only benefit of creating prefixes longer than /64 would be address conservation. Use your mantra and remember that we don't need to conserve space anymore. The benefit of conserving space would be very small compared to the pain of managing a nonstandard subnet prefix.

Nevertheless, you can still choose to use high-order bits from the interface ID part to denote specific systems, services, or networks to make it easier to recognize these IDs. A good and helpful practice when grouping bits is to always do it on a 4-bit boundary. This way, it is much easier to decipher the address because 4 bits represent one hexadecimal digit.

Let's play with some examples to get our brains going. You could group subnets by location and then by service or use type, or the other way round (by service type first and then by location).

So, for instance, with the prefix 2001:db8:1::/48, you have 16 bits for subnetting. You can choose to subnet as follows (L=location, S=service, F=free):

```
Location first:        2001:db8:1:LLLLSSSS FFFFFFFF::/64
Service type first:    2001:db8:1:SSSSLLLL FFFFFFFF::/64
```

Which option you choose depends on whether your main purpose is to optimize routing—in which case, you choose the location identifier first—or whether you want to optimize security rules and ACLs (which are usually based on filters for specific services), in which case you would choose the service identifier first. In some cases, organizations only assign a subnet to a location, and the location further manages the prefix and creates its own address plan. In such a case, you would also choose the location identifier first.

Or you may want to mix these two options. You may have some specific services that you want to filter on at a high level, so you would put identifiers for these services in the highest-order bits of your subnet range, perhaps followed by location bits to optimize the routing within your network, and ending with bits to identify more services.

With the 4 bits used for location and service type in this example, you can create 16 locations and services (2^4). You have to adapt this scheme to the number of locations and services you want represented (and add enough room for growth). Sometimes organizations include a location or service description in their VLAN numbering plans. This could also be reflected in your IPv6 addressing plan to include the 12-bit VLAN ID in the prefix. You can include it in decimal notation (leaving out A–F) or convert it to hexadecimal notation.

These are all general ideas for and input on your creative planning. Take the time to carefully craft your future addressing design, discuss all possible options again and again, have your address concept proposal reviewed by many people—including external consultants—and go over it repeatedly until it feels right. The address design is the foundation for your next-generation network. If you don't get it right and have to change it during the deployment project, this will add costs and delay the project. In the long term, if you live with a suboptimal address design, returning operational costs may be unnecessarily high.

Configuration of interface IDs

How interface IDs are defined depends on the IP address management process that you choose. You can either choose *SLAAC* (stateless address autoconfiguration), where interfaces create interface IDs based on MAC address (EUI-64 format defined in RFC 4291), or with the *privacy option* (as defined in RFC 4941), where the interface ID is randomly generated and changed regularly. You can use DHCPv6 and assign addresses just as you do in IPv4. With DHCPv6, the service may have options to define interface IDs in different ways, so to best secure your hosts, you may not want to start at a low interface ID and sequentially number your interfaces. Instead, you may want to have random interface IDs, because the more random and distributed your interface IDs are, the harder it is to scan them.

If you have a global IPv6 prefix and use a ULA prefix internally, you may want to use the privacy option for the global prefix. This way, users accessing the Internet cannot easily be tracked because their interface ID changes regularly. For the ULA prefix, it's preferable to have fixed addresses assigned to make management, troubleshooting, security, and logging easier. Again, this also depends on whether vendors will provide IP address management solutions that help to deal with this.

One note of caution for users of Microsoft Windows Vista, Windows 7, and Windows Server 2008: when you're using SLAAC, Microsoft has elected to generate random interface IDs by default for nontemporary, autoconfigured IPv6 addresses (including public and link-local addresses), rather than EUI-64-based interface IDs. These are privacy extensions related to RFC 4941. While this behavior is usually fine for clients, it may adversely impact services where SLAAC and randomized interface identifiers are used on servers. Just imagine the impact if the IPv6 address is constantly changing on a web, file, or print server! You can remedy this by using static IPv6 address assignment, DHCPv6, or a documented `netsh` command.

Security Design

Having a strong security design is very important for managing a dual-stacked network. As soon as you introduce IPv6 into your network, you have an additional entry point.

You even have an additional entry point right now, because although you may not have deployed IPv6 yet, you probably have many operating systems in your network that have IPv6 enabled by default (Windows Vista and Windows 7, Windows Server 2008, Linux clients, Macintosh clients, and likely many more). While the operating systems can't get too far as long as you don't have IPv6 routing enabled, they can be very chatty with ND and service location requests, and hackers can use them as a backdoor to your IPv4 network.

So, as a first step of protection before you deploy IPv6, make sure you filter all IPv6 traffic coming into and leaving your network. This includes native IPv6 traffic and tunneled traffic. In addition, it might be wise to monitor and audit IPv6 traffic—specifically ND messages such as router or neighbor advertisements that could be used to configure your clients with incorrect gateway or DNS server information.

Your future security design will have to secure both protocols: you still have your IPv4 security design, and you will have to define an IPv6 security design. If your IPv4 security concept is well designed, it is advisable to align your IPv6 security concept with it. You will have to add protection from attacks that use IPv6-specific mechanisms, such as extension headers, multicast addresses or neighbor discovery messages, SLAAC, and specifically tunnels.

Is IPv6 more secure than IPv4?

One frequently asked question is whether IPv6 is more secure than IPv4. The answer is yes and no, depending on your interpretation.

IPsec is used to secure IPv6, and it has the same features as the version you are using with IPv4 today. In fact, the IPsec you are using today was originally developed for IPv6, but when the need for security became very urgent, it was developed to work with

IPv4 as well. So, in this regard, IPv6 offers the same level of security as IPv4. The main difference is that with IPv4, you have to buy and install some product on your IPv4 hosts to use IPsec. With IPv6, however, IPsec implementation is a mandatory part of every IPv6 stack. In both cases you need to configure it properly in order to work. Thus, from this perspective, you could argue that IPv6 is more secure because implementation is always available. Finally, with IPsec and IPv4, because IPsec requires end-to-end connections, we always face problems when a NAT device is in the way. Since we will not have NATs in an IPv6 network, we avoid this problem. And with IPv4 IPsec, your connections are restricted to gateway-to-gateway and host-to-server, whereas with IPv6 IPsec, you can use any combination to build a secure tunnel.

On the other hand, IPv6 will likely be less secure in the early days of deployment for two reasons. First, the stacks may be buggier than usual because they are all early implementations, and vendors have to wait for market response and incident reports to fix their implementations. So, when planning your project, you should allow for enough time to test stacks and security implementations in your lab before you go to production. The second reason is that we are not very familiar with the new features of IPv6 yet, so we need some time to build experience and find the best ways to secure our IPv6 network and our hosts.

IPv6 security design

When we designed our first networks many years ago, security wasn't a major concern. We added security mechanisms as the networks and the Internet grew and the number of attacks increased. Today we live in a world where hackers are not just geeks that see a challenge in breaking through security mechanisms anymore, but where organized cyber crime becomes a major concern. Designing our next generation network based on IPv6 offers the opportunity to rethink security and finally make it ubiquitous in the environment. A well-designed security concept has the following characteristics:

- Perimeter firewalls secure your network from general network attacks.
- Host firewalls secure your hosts from host- and application-based attacks.

These are good rules for an IPv4 security design, and they are valuable for your IPv6 security design as well. In addition to these rules, you need to consider the potential of the hierarchical address space for new security models. This includes having a well-designed address plan for efficient filtering as well as using multiple addresses on a single interface, which may be used for different applications and also different address types such as link-local addresses, ULAs, and global addresses.

Issues to watch for

Many of the attacks against our IPv4 networks will also be used for IPv6. But we have to take all the new protocol elements into account to fully protect ourselves. The following list describes some possible attacks:

- Attackers can use extension headers to get viruses or other malicious code into your network. Your firewall should allow only the extension headers that are needed and filter all the others. It should also filter extension headers that are illegal or deprecated, and packets with an illegal sequence or unusually long chain of extension headers. Extension headers should be inspected.

- All tunnel mechanisms can be used for attacks. All firewall and intrusion detection/ intrusion prevention systems (IDS/IPS) need to perform deep packet inspection of tunneled packets. Specifically, Teredo might be a good mechanism for attackers to use, as it is almost impossible to efficiently filter its traffic. There is a UDP port used for Teredo—UDP port 3544—but it can easily be changed.

- The new neighbor discovery messages and all ND mechanisms can be used for new types of attacks. Specifically, router advertisements can be used to misconfigure clients on a subnet with illegal prefixes, wrong DNS servers, or default gateway information, for example.

- SLAAC offers new possibilities for attacks. For instance, a device responding to all DAD (duplicate address detection) tests on a link can run an efficient DOS attack because SLAAC clients can then no longer initialize an IPv6 address.

- The all-nodes multicast address of ff02::1 and the all-routers multicast address of ff02::2 can be used to find all hosts and routers on a link.

- The neighbor cache and destination cache on a host can be used to read all connection information and find addresses of peers and other systems in the network.

- If you have an implementation of Mobile IPv6 (MIPv6), be aware that this technology offers many additional points for attacks. Check the MIPv6 specification for security recommendations.

- If you start using end-to-end IPsec encryption on a large scale, it will become more and more difficult to examine packet content.

 For a thorough discussion of IPv6 security concepts, I recommend Scott Hogg's and Eric Vyncke's book *IPv6 Security* (Cisco Press).

Procedures

Your steps to define a new security design may look like this:

1. Make sure everybody participating in the discussion has a good understanding of IPv6 security issues.

2. If you have consultants on board, make sure they understand your internal policies and current security design.

3. Assess your existing security design for what has worked well and possible improvements.

4. Apply what has worked well and your list of improvements to your IPv6 security design, and add all the new options based on IPv6 features.

5. Make sure the design is manageable in a dual-stacked world.

6. Write the IPv6 requirements list for all your security devices.

7. Assess all existing firewalls, IDS, and IPS, as well as any other central security management systems, for their capability and IPv6 compliance.

8. Assess all router operating systems for the correct level of IPv6 support for packet filtering and rate limiting, access control, and control plane protection. Check performance for IPv6 filtering (i.e., determine whether it is done in hardware or in software). The fact that a device does filtering of IPv4 in hardware does not necessarily mean that filtering for IPv6 is also done in hardware. For a dual-stacked environment, evaluate the capacity of all filtering systems to filter on both protocols.

9. Refine your security concept, choose your vendors, define a deployment plan, and test that plan in your lab.

Using directory services for controlling access

While we talk about new designs for future networks, let's explore a new approach that could make a lot of sense in a dual-stacked and multiple-address-per-interface world. We are used to defining access rules based on IP addresses. This can be very limiting, especially when you consider the multiple addresses of IPv6 interfaces and scenarios in which a user wants to access a specific application from different subnets; if we base rules on IP addresses, we have to know about all these subnets and configure rules for each.

A new approach is to base rule definitions on identities in a directory service. After all, we want to control access for specific groups, specific machines, or maybe specific users, depending on what machine they are coming from. With IP-based access rules, this can become very complicated in a dual-stacked or IPv6 world. So, if we instead assigned rules based on identities, controlling access would be a lot easier, and the security device could resolve the rule by querying directory services.

It seems that the market is going this direction. In its latest release, Check Point has an implementation of what it calls *Identity Awareness*, which connects the firewall with Active Directory and matches users and machine identities. Identity Awareness shows IP addresses with a user or machine name and lets you define rules based on any of these properties. You can define a firewall rule for specific users when they send traffic from specific machines, or a firewall rule for a specific user regardless of which machine he sends traffic from.

So, when you design your future network, allow yourself to think in new ways. Directory services are a great example where leveraging an existing, powerful tool can change the operational paradigm of the environment. Especially with the introduction of IPv6, there are many possible connections. For instance, using directory services and a well-designed implementation of Identity Management, you can centralize access control to your DMZ, letting partners, customers, and employees access certain services and displaying content based on who they are. With security devices like Check Point's latest release, you can even add rules based on the same identities.

DNS Design

The basics of DNS (Domain Name System) have not changed. For IPv6 DNS services, you need the following:

- DNS servers that support AAAA ("quad-A") records for 128-bit IPv6 addresses, and the corresponding PTR records. For IPv6 reverse DNS lookups, ip6.arpa is used.
- DNS resolvers (in clients and in DNS servers) that can resolve names and addresses over IPv6 transport.

When a dual-stacked host queries a DNS server for a service name—for instance, when a user enters a URL in the browser—the client will send out two DNS requests: one for an A record and another for a AAAA record. The DNS server may respond with either an A record or a AAAA record, or with both, depending on how it is configured. If the client receives two addresses, it will—based on the default address selection rules (RFC 3484)—prefer native IPv6 over IPv4.

Which transport is used for resolving a name with DNS is independent of the connection that is built. So, for example, Windows XP cannot resolve DNS names over IPv6. A Windows XP client always needs a DNS server that it can reach over IPv4. But when the client is dual-stacked and the DNS server responds with a AAAA record, the Windows XP client can initiate a session over IPv6.

A problem can arise when a client gets a AAAA record but does not have an IPv6 connection or has a very poor one. Because IPv6 stacks are configured to prefer IPv6 over IPv4 by default, the client will try to connect with IPv6. But because it does not have connectivity, there is a long delay until the client eventually reverts to using IPv4 (which it can only do if it got an A record for the same service). In most cases, the user won't understand why it takes so long to access that website and will probably blame the website owner for it.

This "IPv6 brokenness" of clients/browsers is the reason why large dual-stacked websites such as Google and Facebook don't give out AAAA records for their main domain. If you want to access Google or Facebook over IPv6 today, you have to use a v6-specific domain name such as *http://ipv6.google.com*. These large sites cannot accept performance hits due to users on networks with bad IPv6 Internet connectivity. If such a user experiences long timeouts while accessing Google, he will think that Google is responsible for the poor performance, when in fact the timeout stems from the client not being able to connect over IPv6 and waiting to connect over IPv4. Google and other large sites often use DNS whitelisting for ISPs with good IPv6 performance, so they can be sure that users coming from that ISP will have no problems accessing the website over IPv6. Only if you are connected from such a provider will you get a AAAA record for *http://www.google.com*. This was the motivation behind World IPv6 Day, which took place on June 8, 2011. On this date, all major websites enabled the AAAA record for their main domain for 24 hours in order to test what happened, analyze the results, and determine what it takes to improve the situation so they can eventually enable AAAA records for the main domain permanently. To find more information on World IPv6 Day, go to *http://isoc.org/wp/worldipv6day*. The testday was almost uneventful, in that no major problems were encountered. For most users, Internet performance was as usual. Analysis showed that IPv6 brokenness is a declining concern, mainly due to new features in browsers. On that day content available over IPv6 has clearly increased and so has IPv6 Internet traffic over IPv6 increased in general. Many websites that enabled IPv6 for the test day and found no issues decided to leave IPv6 turned on permanently. This accounts for more than 60% of the participating websites. Hopefully we can soon move to an Internet where regular domains can also have AAAA records with no restrictions.

With regard to DNS design, one important point to be aware of is *namespace fragmentation*. When a resolver tries to resolve a name, it will start at the root and follow referrals until it reaches an authoritative name server for the name. If the resolver encounters a name server that is reachable only over a protocol that the resolver can't use, the name cannot be resolved—the DNS query is unsuccessful.

As IPv6 starts being deployed more and more in the Internet, the namespace may get fragmented because there will still be name servers that can be reached only over IPv4, as well as more and more name servers that can be reached only over IPv6. So we need mechanisms to avoid the situation where the resolver chain breaks due to two name servers in the resolution process that do not speak the same "language" (IP version); here are the DNS recommendations (excerpted from RFC 3901) on this topic:

> In order to preserve name space continuity, the following administrative policies are recommended:
>
> - Every recursive name server SHOULD be either IPv4-only or dual stack.
>
>   This rules out IPv6-only recursive servers. However, one might design configurations where a chain of IPv6-only name [servers forwards] queries to a set of dual-stack recursive name [servers] actually performing those recursive queries.
>
> - Every DNS zone SHOULD be served by at least one IPv4-reachable authoritative name server.
>
>   This rules out DNS zones served only by IPv6-only authoritative name servers.
>
> Note: zone validation processes SHOULD ensure that there is at least one IPv4 address record available for the name servers of any child delegations within the zone.

For your integration of IPv6, it is probably a good idea to plan for dual-stacked DNS services, as this offers the best and most flexible protection from fragmentation. With BIND9, you can also configure a dual-stack server. When a recursor needs to look up data in a zone served only by a name server that doesn't speak the same language, it can forward a recursive query to the dual-stack server.

Make sure that you configure AAAA records only when the services are fully reachable over IPv6; otherwise, your clients may experience long timeouts or not reach the service at all. We also have to move away from entering host names only in DNS. A host may be dual-stacked (and have two DNS entries), while some services running on that host may be either IPv4 or IPv6 services. In a large enterprise, it could be prudent for administrative reasons to avoid mixing IPv4 services and IPv6 services on dual-stacked hosts, but rather to place IPv4 services on IPv4 hosts and IPv6 services on IPv6 hosts. At the same time, you have to make sure that all clients that get AAAA records for IPv6-only services can connect over IPv6 to the network where the service resides. If a service is available on both protocols, make sure the IPv6 service gets precedence over the IPv4 service so your traffic can shift to using IPv6 more and more whenever it is available.

There is already a good amount of experience with IPv6 DNS available. Here is a list of RFCs you should check before you spend a lot of time troubleshooting DNS. Your issues may already have been documented:

- RFC 3596: DNS Extensions for IPv6
- RFC 3901: DNS IPv6 Transport Operational Guidelines
- RFC 4074: Common Misbehavior Against DNS Queries for IPv6 Addresses
- RFC 4472: Operational Considerations and Issues with IPv6 DNS
- RFC 4697: Observed DNS Resolution Misbehavior
- RFC 5358: Preventing Use of Recursive Nameservers in Reflector Attacks
- RFC 5452: Measures for Making DNS More Resilient against Forged Answers
- RFC 5855: Nameservers for IPv4 and IPv6 Reverse Zones
- RFC 6195: Domain Name System (DNS) IANA Considerations

 For a good read on DNS in general and specifically on DNS with IPv6, I recommend the following books, both by Cricket Liu and published by O'Reilly: *DNS and BIND*, Fifth Edition, and *DNS and BIND on IPv6*.

Management Concept

The procedures in this area are the same as outlined previously in the section "Security Design" on page 35, and apply to any other subproject:

1. Make sure everybody in the discussion has a good understanding of what the requirements are to manage an IPv6 network.
2. If you have consultants on board, make sure they understand your internal policies, current procedures and tools used to manage your network.
3. Asses all your existing management and troubleshooting strategies for what has worked well and possible improvements.
4. Apply what has worked well and your list of improvements to your IPv6 management concept and add all new options based on IPv6 features.
5. Make sure the design is manageable in a dual-stacked world.
6. Write the IPv6 requirements list for all your management devices.
7. Assess all existing management systems for their IPv6 capability and compliance.
8. Refine your management concept, choose your vendors, define a deployment plan and test it in your lab.

A management system may well understand and manage IPv6 while still communicating over IPv4. In fact, many management systems today don't support IPv6 transport. For example, SNMP may carry information about an IPv6 network element, but the SNMP message may be transported over IPv4. Make sure to test for this behavior and evaluate accordingly. Depending on your situation, you may be doing well with an IPv4-communicating management system as long as you operate in a dual-stack network.

Address Management

With IPv6, you have three options for configuring devices for an IP address. Option one is using SLAAC, in which interfaces autoconfigure an address either based on its MAC identifier (EUI-64) or by using the privacy option, where the interface ID is randomly generated and changed in regular intervals. This interface ID is then combined with routing prefixes learned from router advertisements. The second option is to use DHCPv6, which is very similar to DHCPv4. What is new in DHCPv6 is that it includes an authentication framework. You can also combine these first two configuration options by having interfaces use SLAAC for the address configuration and then sending out DHCP inform requests to get additional configuration from a DHCP server. Or another combination is that clients can use SLAAC to configure an address for one prefix and then go to a DHCPv6 server to get an address for another prefix. The third option is to manually configure interfaces for an IPv6 address. You may want to use this option for servers and routers to make sure you have control over the address.

If you want to populate DNS with the device entries, in the case of SLAAC you will have the clients update DNS (Dynamic DNS). If you are using DHCPv6, you probably want the DHCP server to update DNS. It may be a good idea to secure DNS (DNSsec).

SLAAC is a great and easy way to configure your devices for an IP address if you have a smaller company or if you need to configure networks with frequently changing users, such as public ad-hoc networks (mobile and wireless networks) or areas in your corporate network where you have guests and partners connecting temporarily. SLAAC is also very useful for the configuration of sensors.

In the enterprise area, most customers choose DHCPv6. The reasons are that DHCPv6 offers you more control and *stateful configuration*, which means that you always know which device used which address at a certain time (for security and policy reasons). Servers, routers, switches, firewalls, and similar devices should be statically configured.

Many enterprises use an IPAM suite, or DDI as it is called nowadays. DDI stands for *DNS, DHCP,* and *IPAM.* As of early 2011, there aren't too many production DHCPv6 servers out there. Most vendors have announced their DHCPv6 server for sometime in 2011. Many suites already offer different levels of address management options. It is advisable to work closely with your vendor and find out what his level of IPv6 support is and what his roadmap looks like. Managing a dual-stacked network is quite complex, and you need tools that offer the greatest flexibility and present a clear view on your network devices from different perspectives. You probably want to be able to see which IP addresses are assigned to a specific MAC address, or which IP addresses relate to a specific DNS name, or from a device perspective (how many interfaces, what DNS names, and IP addresses for each). You will need to experiment in your lab to find out which address management product best suits your needs.

The Inevitable Word on NAT

In the 90s, NAT was developed because the IPv4 address space became scarce and IPv6 wasn't ready yet. In other words, NAT was created as a temporary solution to the address problem. But then we got used to it and found many additional advantages in the technology, and in fact, this is what delayed the introduction of IPv6 once it was ready. Here are some of the reasons why people use NATs:

- As an address amplifier (many devices can share one public IP address)
- As a poor man's firewall (the devices behind the NAT are hidden)
- To keep the internal addresses stable even if providers change

As we all know, the firewalling properties of NAT are weak and very easy to replace with a state-of-the-art stateful firewall. NAT was not designed to serve as a firewall, after all. Address amplification is no longer an issue with IPv6, since it was developed to do just that. To keep the internal address space stable, we don't have to use NAT; we can use ULAs (RFC 4193 and RFC 4864).

IPv6 was developed to restore the end-to-end connectivity in the Internet, and the IPv6 world should not use NATs anymore. Avoiding NATs will solve many current issues with applications that require end-to-end connectivity and security (IPsec, Voice over IP, and many others). The percentage of our IT costs that we use to maintain, extend, bypass, and troubleshoot NATs is very high, and if we create NAT-free IPv6 networks, our administrative overhead will significantly decrease, and it will be much easier to create mobile and secure networks.

However, one reason why we will not completely get around using some type of NATs is that it took far too long to introduce IPv6. Originally, the developers planned for IPv6 to be integrated while we still had enough IPv4 address space. This would have allowed for the easy-to-implement dual-stacked approach in most cases.

Now, since the IANA pool is definitely empty and the RIR pools will be exhausted over the course of 2011, all Internet growth will be over IPv6. There are two ways of doing this: a) carriers may use *large-scale NAT* (LSN) to provide IPv4 access to more and more users and b) use some form of translation to provide IPv4 access to IPv6-only users. The downside of the LSN approach is, that once the NAT moves from the edge (home user) to the carrier, many users/organizations will hide behind one IP address, which is not only a performance hit, but maybe even more importantly a security threat (an attack on that IP address will affect a large number of users) and prevent the use of IP-based access control lists, to for instance block addresses that are known to send SPAM. At the same time it is also a limitation to customized marketing and personalized website content display, because all these users coming from one ISP NAT will appear to be coming from one IP address, so all statistical and analytical tools cannot provide more specific information on user behavior. The positive effect of this situation is that for all these users with translation and sitting behind LSN, native IPv6 Internet access will be performing much better, which may be an incentive for content providers to move their content to IPv6.

For a more detailed discussion of NAT, refer to Chapter 3.

Summary

The introduction of IPv6 will cost money. The evolution of our networks always created cost, cost that returns in the form of enabling successful business, efficient communication practices and state-of-the-art applications. This chapter outlined the requirements for a successful planning process. Planning with care and taking the time to tackle all these complex questions is a lot of initial work but it is an important long term gain, because it will create many opportunities to redesign our networks and save a lot of operational cost in the future by enabling an efficient infrastructure.

CHAPTER 3

Integration and Transition Technologies

Transition mechanisms facilitate IPv6 integration by enabling IPv4 and IPv6 to coexist in situations where full native IPv6 is not yet possible. Fundamentally, transition mechanisms let you remove or temporarily avoid the constraints often placed on IPv6 deployment by the existing infrastructure. They allow you to decouple your IPv6 rollout schedule from the IPv6 readiness of the environment.

As the term *transition* implies, these mechanisms are not to be used in the long term. Your main goal is to run an IPv6-only network, meaning that the end-state network would have neither IPv4 enabled nor any transition mechanisms left in the network. An IPv6-only network will be much easier to manage and secure, and much more efficient in routing and administration. But since in most cases you cannot deploy native IPv6 in one big step, transition mechanisms support a phased integration to reach that end goal—they are only to be used temporarily until you can turn on native IPv6. And because IPv4 will coexist with IPv6 for a long time, I prefer to instead call them *integration mechanisms*, as they help you get IPv6 deployed while you're still running IPv4.

Overview of the Integration and Transition Technologies

There is a large and growing number of integration mechanisms. They can be classified as follows:

- Dual-stack
- Tunneling
- Translation

From the 50,000-foot view, this is also the preferred order of leveraging these mechanisms. Since nobody will have a "flag day" transition from IPv4 to IPv6, your network will need to support both protocols simultaneously, and the easiest way to do this is with the dual-stack mechanism. If dual-stack is not possible (for example, because the

ISP does not currently support IPv6, or some expensive devices don't support it and can't be replaced right now), your next choice should be a tunneling solution. Finally, and only if dual-stack and tunneling solutions don't work, you may use a translation mechanism. The translation mechanism is the most complex mechanism with the biggest cost and performance hit, and it often comes with a serious loss of functionality.

The next sections describe the mechanisms available in each category to give you an idea of what is available and some guidance on what's best for your particular environment and deployment plan. On the path from an IPv4 network to your future IPv6 network, you will go through different stages of IPv6 deployment, each stage possibly requiring different integration mechanisms. This is explained in more detail in the section "High-Level Concept" on page 18, in Chapter 2.

Available Mechanisms

The following sections provide an overview of the currently available integration mechanisms, sorted by category. Some of these mechanisms continue to be refined by the engineering community, but most of them have already been used in many production deployments worldwide.

Dual-Stack

Dual-stack is nothing new. If you were a Novell NetWare shop, you ran IPX (internetwork packet exchange) along with IPv4 on the same interface; or if you have Macs, you are running AppleTalk along with IPv4. In this dual-stack approach, we are running two versions of IP on the same interface.

 When we talk about dual-stack, we talk about using IPv6 natively (no use of transition mechanisms such as tunneling or translation). In the dual-stack approach we use native IPv6 together with IPv4. If we run a network which doesn't need IPv4 anymore, we call it an IPv6-only network.

A dual-stacked node can support both IPv4 and IPv6 on the same interface. The interface has one (and possibly a secondary) IPv4 address and, normally, multiple IPv6 addresses. An application can use either IP version as a transport, depending on availability, configuration, and operational policies. In most cases, the choice between using IPv4 or IPv6 is based on DNS configuration (see the section "DNS Design" on page 39, in Chapter 2, for more details).

The dual-stack approach is the most flexible integration mechanism, as it supports legacy IPv4 applications and at the same time allows you to deploy new, possibly IPv6-only, applications. It also makes it easy to turn off IPv4 once it isn't required anymore. You can configure an IPv6 infrastructure that is independent of IPv4, even if you run it on the same physical network. Keep in mind, though, that you can choose this approach only if you have sufficient IPv4 address space. As soon as a lack of IPv4 addresses drives your project, you will probably have to look for other solutions.

 Whenever you can, choose native IPv6. Only if that doesn't work for some reason you should start looking into other integration mechanisms.

Obviously, in most cases the dual-stack mechanism is combined with another mechanism, such as tunneling. Dual-stack does not mean *everything* in the network is dual-stack; otherwise, you wouldn't need it in the first place. If everything was dual-stack, you could turn off IPv4. So, to clarify, dual-stack means that parts of your network and groups of hosts are dual-stacked, while others are mostly IPv4-only and some may be IPv6-only. Your clients may be dual-stacked—able to use IPv6 for new applications while simultaneously supporting legacy applications that are IPv4-only. Clients may also need IPv4 in order to use IPv4 resources outside your corporate domain.

The reason you may need to support legacy IPv4 applications is that some of them have the layer 3 stack incorporated into the compiled application code and cannot support IPv6 without a complete overhaul—which may be impossible, especially with orphaned applications. This means that there are applications out there that can never be migrated to support IPv6 but may still be needed for many years to come. At the same time, the number of IPv6-enabled applications is rising, so there will be a gradual shift of IPv4 traffic to IPv6 traffic. At some point in the future, though, you will be able to turn off IPv4 completely.

Dual-stack requires more resources than a single protocol approach for the following reasons:

- The network bandwidth is shared and its use prioritized between the two protocols. In most cases total traffic does not increase substantially, but some capacity planning might be a good idea, especially if you are adding new IPv6 services to your network.
- Hosts need resources for two independent TCP/IP stacks.
- You may need two IGP routing protocols.
- Routers share resources for holding routing information and performing SP (shortest path) calculations and lookups for each protocol.
- You need two security concepts. Security requirements and administration will be different for IPv4 and IPv6.

- Security devices need more resources for handling two protocol versions. Hardware forwarding devices, for example, support a limited number of ACLs, which could be too limited to handle ACLs for IPv6 in addition to the IPv4 ACLs.

- Operational and management tools must support two protocols in provisioning, monitoring, and troubleshooting.

In spite of these complications, the advantages you get from the flexibility a dual-stack approach offers probably outweigh the disadvantages.

MPLS

MPLS (multiprotocol label switching) is not an IPv6 transition mechanism, but it can be used nicely in such a scenario. MPLS sits between layer 2 and layer 3 in the protocol stack and tunnels network layer traffic using a set of labels. If you have an MPLS backbone, you can simply label IPv6 traffic.

There are two flavors to use MPLS as an IPv6 transition mechanism. The first, called 6PE (RFC 4798), is a native IPv6 tunnel over an IPv4 MPLS core. In this variation, IPv6 packets are encapsulated in MPLS frames and switched across the MPLS core based on two labels. No changes are required in the operation of the MPLS core. Dual-stack edge routers (*provider edge*, or PE, and *customer edge*, or CE) use multiprotocol BGP to exchange IPv6 routing information and corresponding labels to IPv4 endpoints.

The other flavor, called 6VPE (RFC 4659), is an IPv6 layer 3 VPN over MPLS. In this case, IPv6 packet labeling is IPv6 VPN–specific. A second IPv4 label is appended for forwarding over the MPLS core, which allows for isolation of IPv6 transport for specific customers or services. By comparison, 6PE is similar to a single, global VPN.

Whenever you have MPLS available, choose one of these flavors depending on your requirements. MPLS is your best choice. It is widely implemented and deployed, and has a proven successful track record.

Tunneling

Generally, tunnels allow packets of a certain protocol to be encapsulated in a header of another protocol in order to traverse certain parts of a network. So, in our example, you can transport IPv6 packets over an IPv4 backbone by encapsulating the IPv6 packet in an IPv4 header. The tunnel endpoints manage the encapsulation and decapsulation. Tunnels are mostly used in the edge-to-core approach, usually combined with dual-stack or to connect IPv6 islands. For instance, you could have a tunnel from the edge of your network to the edge of your core, the core being native IPv6, or you could have a tunnel from edge to edge across an IPv4 core.

You should implement tunnels only if native IPv6 is not possible. Right now, the IP protocol 41 tunneling (41 is the protocol value for IPv6 encapsulated in IPv4) is the most used version, because the Internet and corporate networks are IPv4 networks. Over time, as the number of IPv6 networks exceeds the number of IPv4 networks, we can expect the reverse to happen: IPv4 packets will begin to be tunneled in IPv6 packets. IPv6 is expected to enhance the performance of the Internet, but we will not see that improvement until most forwarding takes place in native IPv6.

You can configure tunnels either manually or automatically. Manually configured tunnels work well in less dynamic environments, where you connect two or more networks that are in a controlled environment. If there are too many networks, or if the networks are very dynamic, the administrative burden of managing the tunnels may become too big. Automatic tunnels ease administration. Usually, the IPv4 destination address for the tunnel endpoint is embedded as part of the end node's IPv6 address. This will be discussed in the upcoming sections on 6to4, Teredo, and ISATAP tunneling. In other cases, you can find the destination tunnel address by querying DNS.

6to4

The 6to4 mechanism defined in RFC 3056 (and illustrated in Figure 3-1) has been the recommended automatic tunneling mechanism for a long time. 6to4 requires one globally routable IPv4 address to operate. A *6to4 router* connects a domain configured with the 6to4 prefix (we call this a *6to4 network*) with another 6to4 network or with the IPv6 Internet. 6to4 uses a reserved prefix—2002::/16.

16 bit	32 bit	16 bit	64 bit
2002	IPv4 Address	Subnet ID	Interface ID

Figure 3-1. Format of the 6to4 address

Embedding the global IPv4 address in the prefix makes automatic tunneling possible. The 6to4 prefix of 2002::/16, combined with the 32-bit IPv4 address, creates a /48 prefix. This leaves 16 bits for intrasite subnets. A public IPv4 address of 62.2.84.115 would create the 6to4 prefix of 2002:3e02:5473::/48 (the IPv4 address represented in hexadecimal).

Figure 3-2 shows the 6to4 communication.

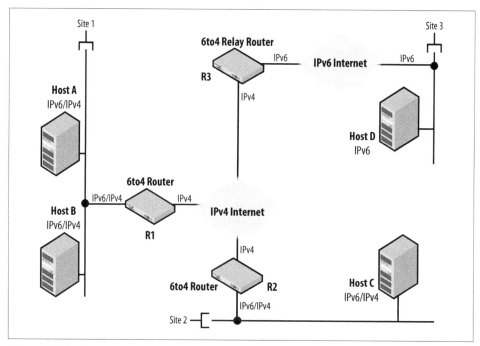

Figure 3-2. 6to4 communication

Figure 3-2 shows two 6to4 routers, R1 and R2, at the border of two different 6to4 sites. The 2002::/16 prefix used in each site is the 6to4 prefix, and the 32 bits following the 2002::/16 represent the IPv4 address of the public interface of each of the 6to4 routers. A 6to4 router requires at least one public IPv4 address. All hosts within each 6to4 site are configured for addresses within their 6to4 prefix, which is:

```
R1: 2002:IPv4addressR1::/48
R2: 2002:IPv4addressR2::/48
```

The nodes on the network are provisioned either by router advertisements or through DHCPv6.

For connections between the two 6to4 sites, the tunneling is automatic. Let's say R1 gets a packet from a host in its network with a destination for a host in 6to4 network 2. R1 can identify the destination network as a 6to4 network based on the 2002::/16 prefix, and being a 6to4 router, it knows that the IPv4 address of the tunnel endpoint is part of the IPv6 prefix in the destination address field. R1 extracts the 32 bits following the 2002::/16 prefix from the destination address field in the IPv6 header to build an IPv4 header with its own IPv4 source address and the extracted IPv4 address of R2 in the destination address field; then, it sends the IPv4 encapsulated IPv6 packet over the IPv4 infrastructure. R2 receives the IPv4 packet, decapsulates it by stripping off the IPv4 header, performs an IPv6 routing lookup, and forwards the IPv6 packet to its final destination.

For connections with the native IPv6 Internet, the situation is a little more complex and a *6to4 relay* is needed. Automatic tunneling doesn't work in this scenario, since there is no IPv4 address embedded in the IPv6 destination address. So, for example, how can R1 find the relay router R3? There are two possible mechanisms. RFC 3068 defines an anycast address to find 6to4 relays, or the relay could be preconfigured on R1. The way back from the native IPv6 network to the 6to4 network is found by R3 advertising the 6to4 prefix of 2002::/16 into the native IPv6 network.

The 6to4 mechanism has some limitations:

- There is no guarantee that every native IPv6 device in the Internet will find a working route to reach 6to4 hosts.
- There are issues with delegating reverse DNS records (translating IPv6 addresses into host names). The conventional address delegation procedures do not work for 6to4 as in this case, the DNS records would have to reflect the IPv4 address delegation (RFC 5158). This causes some issues that have not been fully resolved.
- For connections with native IPv6 Internet, routing is not under your own administrative control, so you must depend on public deployment of 6to4 relays.

The last bullet point is one of the main problems with 6to4. ISPs were expected to deploy 6to4 relays in large numbers, but this has not been the case. So 6to4 performance and routing are not optimal, which is one reason why 6to4 has not really taken off and will now probably be replaced by 6rd (described in the next section).

You can use 6to4 if you have no global IPv6 prefix (yet) but want to communicate with the IPv6 Internet. It doesn't make sense to use 6to4 if you already have a global IPv6 prefix, since you'd probably prefer a mechanism that uses your own IPv6 address. You can also use 6to4 in a network with NAT if the NAT box has a full implementation of an IPv6 router, and the public IPv4 address of the outermost NAT box is used to build the 6to4 prefix.

As one of the older tunnel mechanisms, 6to4 is widely supported in code. You can find it in almost any equipment and operating system. There is an ongoing discussion in the IETF working group about deprecating the 6to4 anycast address and moving 6to4 to historic. RFC 6343, "Advisory Guidelines for 6to4 Deployment" offers guidelines for using the protocol. If you are deploying now or will in the near future, you may want to use 6rd, a variant of 6to4.

IPv6 sites can somewhat improve the experience of those clients that still use the anycast 6to4 relay address by installing 6to4 relays, which encapsulate any IPv6 traffic to the 2002::/16 prefix, and send it directly to the destination router over IPv4. This would help decrease the latency on the reverse path. The forward path is not in the server's control, and usually under only limited client control. Those who deploy the client side could also improve the experience by installing IPv6-connected 6to4 relays to improve the latency for the traffic in the forward direction.

6rd

6rd was developed by Free.fr, an ISP in France. Within only five weeks in 2007, Free enabled IPv6 Internet access for 1.5 million residential customers. The company managed to do this by basing its mechanism on 6to4, which (as mentioned previously) is code that you find in all devices and operating systems. Free modified 6to4 slightly to make it more suitable for ISP requirements. 6rd does not use the 6to4 prefix of 2002::/16, but instead uses the ISP's global unicast prefix. If you are interested in how Free accomplished this integration, you can read the description in RFC 5569. Because the mechanism was easy to deploy and seemed useful, it was adopted by the IETF working group and is standardized today in RFC 5969, "IPv6 Rapid Deployment on IPv4 Infrastructures (6rd)."

6rd is a dynamic tunneling protocol that provides IPv6 access to native IPv6 islands connected over an IPv4 backbone (usually, the ISP IPv4 network). 6rd builds on the principles and experiences of 6to4, and is similar to it at a very high level. The mapping between the IPv6 and IPv4 addresses within the ISP network enables the automatic determination of the IPv4 tunnel endpoints from the IPv6 prefix. However, there are some important differences:

- 6to4 uses a predefined prefix (2002::/16), while 6rd can be tailored to use the provider-allocated prefixes. This eases the later transition to native IPv6 within the backbone and solves the routing issues in the Internet.
- The concept of relay is present in 6rd as well, however, 6rd relays have IPv6 addresses within the allocation of the organization and IPv4 anycast addresses selected by the organization. With 6rd, the organization providing the service is in full control of the relay resources and can manage the asymmetrical routing problems plaguing 6to4.

Figure 3-3 shows the construction of the prefix for the end nodes connected using 6rd.

n bits	o bits	m bits	128 - n - o - m
SP Prefix	IPv4 Address	Subnet ID	Interface ID

Figure 3-3. Format of the 6rd address

The 6rd prefix is taken from the public IPv6 unicast space, so each provider can choose the prefix from his ISP allocation. This way, 6rd operates fully under the ISP's administrative control, and all 6rd hosts are reachable from anywhere through regular routing mechanisms. If the provider has a /32 prefix, and 24 bits of the IPv4 address are used (the unique bits of all IPv4 addresses within a given 6rd domain; see the RFC), the customer gets a /56 (32 + 24).

The client part of 6rd runs on the CPE (customer premises equipment) devices connecting the customer network with the Internet. These CPE devices serve native IPv6 addresses (according to the prefix) to the end hosts in the customer network. To send IPv6 packets to the Internet, the CPE acts like the tunnel server, encapsulating them into protocol 41 and forwarding them over IPv4. The tunnel destination in the IPv4 tunnel header depends on the destination IPv6 address. If the destination IPv6 address is within the 6rd domain (i.e., the SP prefix is the same), then the CPE will construct the tunnel endpoint address based on the configured IPv4 prefix for the domain and the IPv4 address extracted from the destination IPv6 address. If the destination IPv6 address is outside the domain, the CPE will send the protocol 41 packets to an explicitly configured IPv4 address of a *border relay router* (BR). The border relays are routers on the "Internet" side of the local backbone and have native IPv6 connectivity to the Internet. They will decapsulate the tunneled packets and forward the IPv6 packets to the destination.

For the return packets, the routing for the 6rd-enabled IPv6 prefixes needs to direct the IPv6 packets from the Internet to a BR router. The BR router will deduce the IPv4 tunnel destination address based on the IPv4 address taken from the IPv6 destination address.

The 6rd mechanism allows for stateless and scalable deployment with predictable performance characteristics. There are many large-scale deployments based on 6rd, so, if your deployment involves IPv6 islands over an IPv4 backbone, this would be a proven and scalable way to go.

ISATAP

ISATAP stands for *Intrasite Automatic Tunnel Addressing Protocol* and is defined in RFC 5214. As its name implies, ISATAP was created to connect IPv6 hosts in an IPv4-only routed network, where you can't deploy IPv6 routers for the moment.

The ISATAP tunneling mechanism works just like 6to4, except with ISATAP the tunnel endpoint is created within the host. So, whereas 6to4 is a router-to-router tunnel, ISATAP is a host-to-host tunnel. The ISATAP driver on the interface is the tunnel endpoint. The application sends an IPv6 packet to some IPv6 destination. Before the packet leaves the interface to get onto the IPv4 network, the ISATAP driver encapsulates the IPv6 packet in an IPv4 header and sends it over the IPv4 infrastructure.

How does the ISATAP driver know the IPv4 destination address for the tunnel header? The IPv4 address of the interface is contained in the last 32 bits of the ISATAP IPv6 address. So, in other words, the ISATAP driver takes the 32 bits from the IPv6 destination address and knows that this is the IPv4 address of the destination interface. The packet arrives at the destination as an IPv4 packet, and the ISATAP driver strips off the IPv4 header and forwards the IPv6 packet internally to the application.

Figure 3-4 shows how the IPv4 address is embedded in the last 32 bits of the IPv6 address. ISATAP works with both private and public IPv4 addresses, and the address contains an identifier to distinguish them (0000 for private addresses and 0200 for public addresses). 5efe is the IANA identifier indicating that this is an IPv6 address with an embedded IPv4 address.

64 bits	32 bits	32 bits
IPv6 prefix	00 00 5e fe (private)	IPv4 address
	02 00 5e fe (public)	

Figure 3-4. Format of the ISATAP address

Let's assume the network prefix is 2001:db8:10:3a::/64. If the node's IPv4 address is 62.2.84.115, the ISATAP address is 2001:db8:10:3a:200:5efe:62.2.84.115. Alternatively, you can convert the IPv4 address to hexadecimal format and write 2001:db8:10:3a:200:5efe:3e02:5473.

So the ISATAP mechanism allows the routing of IPv6 packets within an IPv4-only network. Each host queries an *ISATAP router* within the site to obtain address and routing information. Packets sent to the IPv6 Internet are routed via the ISATAP router, and packets destined for other hosts within the same site are tunneled directly to the destination.

The ISATAP router within the enterprise has direct connectivity to IPv6 Internet. It decapsulates the packet and forwards it to the IPv6 Internet. On the way back, the IPv6 packets from the Internet will hit the ISATAP router, and the router will encapsulate the IPv6 packet into protocol 41 and send it directly to the destination host, using the IPv4 address within the IPv6 address of the destination.

This approach offers a relatively simple-to-enable tunneling mechanism in an IPv4-only infrastructure. All you need to do is to configure isatap.<*yourdomainname*> to be the IPv4 address of your ISATAP router. The hosts that support the protocol will query the DNS name during bootup and enable ISATAP automatically.

You might use ISATAP if you are bound to an IPv4-only routed network but want to open access to the IPv6 Internet for your internal IPv6 users, who are typically dispersed across different subnets. ISATAP makes this access possible without requiring an IPv6 routing infrastructure.

ISATAP is implemented and enabled by default on Windows operating systems. The Linux implementation must be installed separately (isatapd), and FreeBSD has ISATAP support by means of the KAME protocol stack. For MacOS X users, there is a pre-alpha version of the ISATAP client.

Teredo

The 6to4 tunneling mechanism can be used only if you have a public IPv4 address, and ISATAP does not work through NAT either. But the reality is that most residential users sit behind a NAT, so Teredo was developed to allow clients behind a NAT to tunnel packets over an IPv4 infrastructure (RFC 4380, updated by RFC 5991). The way Teredo does this is by tunneling the packets in UDP so they can traverse the NAT gateway. UDP messages can be translated by most NATs and can traverse multiple layers of NATs. The packets are encapsulated at the client and sent to a *Teredo server*, which is responsible for the initial configuration of the Teredo tunnel. The clients must be pre-configured with the address of the Teredo server. Teredo communication will then go through a *Teredo relay*. The Teredo server is used only to provide an IPv6 address to the client and to discover the best Teredo relay for that communication. A Teredo client learns about other Teredo clients on its own IPv4 network by using the IPv4 multicast address 224.0.0.253.

Figure 3-5 shows the structure of a Teredo address. The first 32 bits are the prefix that has been assigned to the Teredo service—the 2001::/32. The next 32 bits are used for the IPv4 address of the Teredo server. The 16-bit flags field defines address types and the NAT type used. The port bits contain the Teredo port. Teredo servers are listening on port 3544 (configurable). The last 32 bits contain the IPv4 address of the Teredo client.

32 bits	32 bits	16 bits	16 bits	32 bits
2001	Server IPv4 address	Flags	Port	Client IPv4 address

Figure 3-5. Format of the Teredo address

Figure 3-6 shows how the Teredo client connects to the Teredo server, which configures the tunnel setup and chooses the best Teredo relay. The NAT gateway is traversed with a IPv4-UDP tunnel. Teredo works with different types of cone NATs, but usually doesn't work with symmetric NATs (for more information, see RFC 5389, "Session Traversal Utilities for NAT").

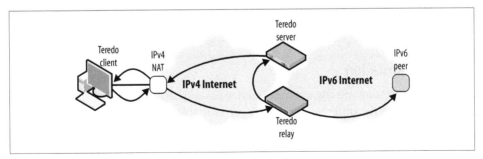

Figure 3-6. Teredo communication

Teredo has more overhead than other tunneling mechanisms and favors robustness over performance. So, if you can choose native IPv6, 6rd, or ISATAP, don't choose Teredo. Over time, more NAT environments will support 6to4 or 6rd (or run on boxes with IPv6 router functionality) and IPv6 connectivity will become more common, so Teredo will be used less and less.

 If you want to see the relation of native traffic versus tunneled traffic in the Internet, check the Google statistics at *http://www.google.com/intl/en/ipv6/statistics*. It shows clearly that tunneled traffic is decreasing while native IPv6 traffic makes up the largest part of total IPv6 traffic.

Besides current Windows operating systems, Teredo is not implemented very widely. There is a Linux implementation (miredo), but it needs to be installed separately in most of the distributions.

Teredo suffers from an issue similar to 6to4 anycast: the unpredictable user experience. To help improve the Teredo user experience, sites can install Teredo relays. Teredo is considered to lower the overall security of a network because it bypasses security controls, allows for unsolicited traffic, and is difficult to track. If your design does not rely on Teredo, you might consider blocking it at the perimeter.

Tunnel broker

The tunnel broker could be considered a sort of virtual IPv6 ISP. It sets up and manages IPv6 connectivity on behalf of IPv6 clients, so it has less impact on internal administration than the other mechanisms described.

When a client (a host or a router) connects to the tunnel broker, the tunnel broker sets up a connection to tunnel servers and assigns the tunnel endpoint and DNS records for the endpoints. Tunnel servers are dual-stack routers, connected to the global Internet.

The tunnel broker specification leaves room for individual implementation. There are many public tunnel broker services available. In many cases, when you register for a tunnel broker service, you can download the scripts that you need to configure your environment. Tunnel brokers are designed to be used in smaller sites or for single users. Using them is a good way to get started with your own private lab, as long as your ISP doesn't support IPv6.

NAT and Translation

NAT and translation are the most debated areas of IPv6 deployment scenarios. This section discusses the different forms of NAT available for the IPv4 address depletion problem and the integration of IPv6.

NAT terminology

To cover these NAT-related mechanisms, we have to extend our NAT terminology. The type of NAT we have been using to date translates private addresses in the customer's site or home into one or more public IPv4 addresses to go out to the Internet. The NAT replaces the packet's private IPv4 address and replaces it with its public IPv4 address. NAT does more than just that in order to provide always-on connectivity to many devices, it not just maps devices and addresses, but also uses ports for each address. There are 65,636 available port numbers each for UDP and TCP, many of which are unused. So NAT actually maps the internal private address and the port number to the outside public address and port number. This way, it can map a large number of sessions for each public address. This type of NAT usually sits at the customer edge and runs on the CPE. We call this legacy form of NAT *NAT44*.

NAT44 has been used for many years. Its main purpose has always been to extend the lifespan of the limited IPv4 address space. IPv6 was designed to overcome the address limitations and therefore is supposed to work without NATs. Even though the goal is to run IPv6 networks without any type of NAT, the fact that we waited too long for IPv6 deployment and are now running out of IPv4 address space will force us to continue using this type of transition technology to deal with the Internet's exponential growth. The problem is that if new Internet users simply get IPv6 addresses, they will not be able to access the still predominantly IPv4-accessible web content. So the IETF working groups decided to define standard translation methods to prevent the industry from developing an ungovernable variety of nonstandard methods.

Some of the new NAT scenarios used these days are necessary to overcome the IPv4 address problem, especially on the ISP side. Although they can't be considered an IPv6 transition mechanism, I describe them here to help you work with your ISP to identify what type and quality of Internet connectivity he offers.

Large-Scale NAT

As providers run out of IPv4 addresses and cannot cover Internet growth with IPv4, they have to deploy IPv6. But users still want to be dual-stacked so they can access IPv4 content on the Internet. So why not NAT the IPv4 part of the Internet connection? This lets users access IPv6 content over IPv6 but still get to IPv4 content over their NAT-ed IPv4 connection.

You can achieve this by using *Large-Scale NAT*, or LSN (sometimes also called *Carrier-Grade NAT*, or CGN), or NAT444. LSN means we add another layer of NAT to the NAT44 by adding a NAT44 inside the ISP's network. Traditional NAT44 is between the customer network and the ISP network. LSN is within the ISP network, and allows the ISP to assign a private IPv4 address to the customers, not a public one. In other words, the traditional customer-side NAT now translates from private IPv4 inside to private IPv4 outside. Figure 3-7 shows this relationship in a diagram.

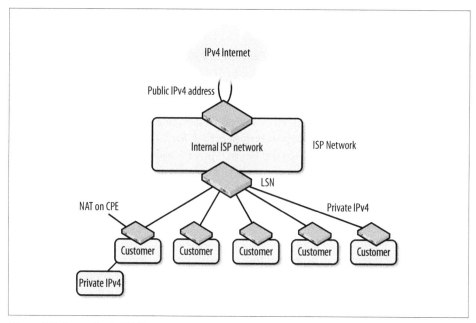

Figure 3-7. Large-Scale NAT

At the bottom of Figure 3-7, we see the traditional NAT connecting a customer's privately addressed networks through NAT with the provider network. In this NAT444 scenario, the translation is from private IPv4 to private IPv4. This allows the ISP to connect many customers through a single public IPv4 address on the outside.

So let's follow a packet. It originates inside the customer site. Its address is converted from private inside to a private address from within the LSN. When leaving the ISP network, it gets the public address assigned to the outside interface of the LSN. The packet goes through address translation and port mapping twice. This mechanism is called NAT444 because it only translates IPv4 to IPv4, with the goal to expand the address space. The advantage here is that you can achieve this mostly with current equipment and implementations.

Time will tell how well this scales with large numbers of users. The processing required for all the translations and mappings for a large number of users will have its limits, which are yet to be determined. There may also be issues with overlapping private space, if an organization uses the same range internally as the provider within the LSN. Another problem might occur if customers connected to the same LSN want to send traffic to each other. Their packets may have to be routed to the outside and come back with a public IPv4 source address; otherwise, they may be filtered by traditional ACLs based on their private source address.

One potentially major pitfall is if somebody successfully attacks the public ISP IPv4 address, it means that not just one customer, but all customers using that LSN IPv4 address, will be affected. It may also prevent the use of IP-based access control lists to, for instance, block addresses that are known to send spam. Another consideration is that all these customers share a fixed pool of ports, so fewer and fewer ports will be available as the number of customers increases. Applications that use a large number of multiple simultaneous sessions—such as Google Maps or iTunes, to name just a couple of examples—will fail. Finally, this approach limits customized marketing and personalized website content display, because all these users coming from one ISP NAT will appear to be coming from one IP address, so all statistical and analytical tools will be unable to provide more specific information on user behavior.

NAT464

Another option is to deploy IPv6-only between the customer edge and the provider network. Known as NAT464, this method requires translation from IPv4 to IPv6 at the customer edge and, again, translation from IPv6 to IPv4 at the LSN. This obviously reduces the need for IPv4 addresses on the provider side. Translation becomes more difficult, as translation across protocols (from IPv4 to IPv6) is more complex than address translation within one protocol family. Furthermore, NAT444 is widely implemented and available, while implementations for NAT464 are not so widespread.

The main disadvantage of this type of translation in general is that, besides the fact that a NAT device is always a bottleneck, when you have to translate IPv6 to IPv4, you lose all the advanced features of IPv6 because they cannot be translated to IPv4. So, for instance, if the packet has extension headers, not all the information can be translated into IPv4 options.

DS-Lite

DS-Lite is a mechanism that allows for IPv6-only connection between the customer site and the LSN, but instead of translating from IPv4 to IPv6 and vice versa as in NAT464, the IPv4 packets are tunneled to the LSN, so no translation needs to be performed. The trick here is to ensure that source addresses are unique. If many customers using private RFC 1918 addresses connect, their source address isn't distinguishable anymore. DS-Lite solves this problem by linking the IPv4 source address with the unique IPv6 address used for the tunnel.

DS-Lite performs a little better than NAT444 or NAT464, because it has only one layer of NAT. The disadvantage is that single users can no longer be identified by their IP address.

Figure 3-8 shows the private customer network connected to the ISP private network through an IPv6 tunnel. The NAT maps the combination of the IPv6 source address, IPv4 source address, and port to the outside IPv4 address and port.

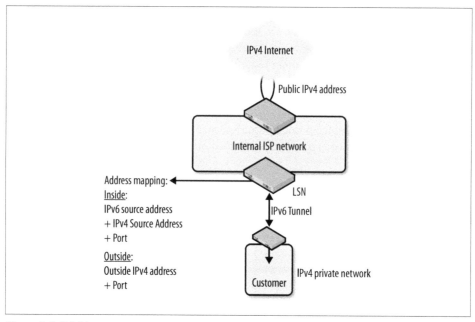

Figure 3-8. DS-Lite

Stateless NAT64

Stateless NAT64 provides a mechanism that translates IPv6 packets into IPv4 packets and vice versa. It is based on RFC 6144, which defines a framework for IPv4/IPv6 translation and provides an overview and discussion of all possible scenarios.

For the stateless mechanism, the translation information is carried in the address itself combined with configuration information in the translator. The translator does not need to maintain state. So this mechanism supports end-to-end transparency and has better scalability than stateful translation.

The disadvantage of this mechanism is that it cannot be used to connect IPv4 networks to the IPv6 Internet, because it is a 1:1 address mapping, which doesn't work in this scenario because there are (will be) way too many IPv6 addresses in the IPv6 Internet to be mapped to IPv4 addresses. So, in this case, you will have to use a stateful translation mechanism, discussed next.

Stateful NAT64 and DNS64

This approach is for scenarios in which users have IPv6 addresses but need to connect to IPv4 networks and the IPv4 Internet. One or more public IPv4 addresses are assigned to the translator to be shared among the IPv6 clients. When stateful NAT64 is used with DNS64, no changes are usually required in the IPv6 client or the IPv4 server. To

---

have support for DNS64, use BIND 9.8.0. Stateful NAT64 is specified in RFC 6146, and DNS64 in RFC 6147.

Figure 3-9 shows how stateful NAT64 with DNS64 works.

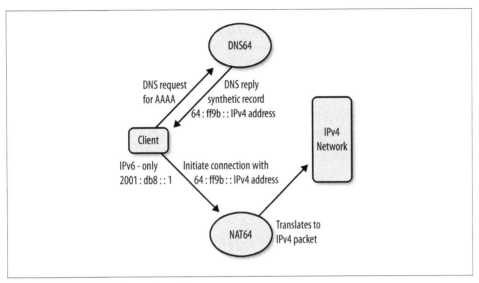

Figure 3-9. Stateful NAT64 with DNS64

The IPv6 client sends a DNS AAAA request to the DNS64 server for a certain service name. If the name server has a AAAA record, it will pass the information and the client will connect over IPv6. If the DNS64 server does not have a AAAA record because it is an IPv4-only service, it finds the corresponding A record and creates a synthetic record. The name server uses the well-known prefix of 64:ff9b::/96 and inserts the IPv4 address it learned from the A record into the 32 low-order bits of the IPv6 address. So, if the A record was 203.10.100.2, the IPv6 address would be 64:ff9b::203.10.100.2.

When the client initializes a connection to this address, it will be routed through the NAT64 gateway. This gateway uses an IPv4 address from its pool with an associated port number, creates a mapping entry for the two addresses, translates the IPv6 header into an IPv4 header (using the translation mechanisms described in RFC 6145), and sends the packet to the destination IPv4 address learned from the IPv6 address.

This has been tested and works for most applications. Problems arise when IPv4 addresses are embedded in applications or when IPv4 literals are used. The best solution is for application developers to stick to using fully qualified domain names (FQDNs) in applications instead of IP addresses. A variety of vendors have implemented stateful NAT64 with DNS64, and large mobile providers are doing trials. In the mobile world, this mechanism may be preferable because it uses less power on the mobile client (battery) than a dual-stack client.

NAT-PT

An early translation mechanism, *NAT-PT* (network address translation/protocol translation) was defined in RFC 2766 and later deprecated in RFC 4966. It used stateless IP/ICMP translation algorithms (SIIT), which are defined in RFC 6145. With translation the header is translated to the header of the other protocol. So a translator takes all the information in an IPv6 header and replaces the IPv6 header with an IPv4 header, while copying and translating all information from IPv6 to IPv4 or vice versa. NAT-PT was designed to be used with DNS application layer gateways.

NAT-PT tried to solve all aspects of translation in one solution, by defining the translation from v4 to v6 (NAT46) and vice versa, from v6 to v4 (NAT64). This created significant complexity and many serious issues. The simpler, more scalable solution used today drops the NAT46 functionality and uses the NAT64 functionality.

And again, no matter what is defined in the future, be aware that translating across protocol families is very limiting. Translating from IPv4 is not that difficult, but when you translate an IPv6 header with extension headers to IPv4, you can lose a lot of information.

How Can IPv6 Clients Reach IPv4 Content?

Due to the empty IPv4 pool, more and more clients and also content providers may find themselves in the position of setting up IPv6-only systems and having to enable some mechanisms to provide access to IPv4-only systems.

So here is a summary of the aforementioned mechanisms that can help in such a situation. The options are:

* LSN, two layers of NAT44, which is what we call NAT444
* DS-Lite, NAT44 at CPE, plus NAT44 at ISP, connected by IPv6 tunnel
* NAT64/DNS64

Whether we like NAT or not, there seems to be no way around it. But which option is the best? If you know that one NAT can be very difficult, degrades performance, and creates issues with applications that may break, it's logical to assume that two layers of NAT—as in NAT444—is even worse. And security is a big concern, because many customers will be coming from one single IPv4 address, which makes it an attractive attack target. So using NAT444 is probably not the best choice.

If we choose NAT44 with DS-Lite, we only have one layer of NAT, so this is definitely preferable. And DS-Lite allows you to use traditional NAT44, which is widely implemented. To access the IPv6 Internet, clients need to be dual-stacked, with an IPv4 stack to access the IPv4 Internet and an IPv6 stack to get to the IPv6 Internet. The gradual move of the client traffic to IPv6 content is a natural one, and requires managing both protocols on the client side.

NAT64 is also a useful option for supporting transition and legacy applications. There are fewer implementations right now and people don't have much experience with it, but this may change soon. This is definitely an option to watch, and maybe even one we should be pushing more vendors and operating systems to support. The advantage of NAT64 is that the client is IPv6-only from the beginning, so the transition to native IPv6 for services that are already reachable over IPv6 is a natural one. There is only one protocol in the access network from the beginning, and translation is used only to access IPv4 content.

Load Balancing

The lack of globally routable IPv4 addresses presents an opposite challenge on the service provider side. For example, if you want to build a new data center, you may not be able to get public IPv4 address space. This means that to ensure you have enough public IP address space, you may want to choose IPv6 as the protocol inside the data center. But can you sell data center space with IPv6-only access? This is probably not an economically viable business model right now!

There are two potential options to cover this scenario:

- Use NAT46 (the opposite of NAT64), the part that was dropped from the NAT-PT specification
- Use load balancers

For the NAT46 choice, there are currently no specifications. There are some proposals, but the general feeling is that it is too complex to map the IPv6 space to the smaller IPv4 space for the sessions initiated by IPv4 hosts. But it is possible that such a mechanism may be developed once this requirement becomes more obvious. On the other hand, the load balancer choice is probably doable right now and a good short-term solution, since load balancers are essentially mandatory pieces of equipment for the frontend in data centers anyway. Several vendors offer high-performance load balancers that support many different mechanisms and can be used in most scenarios. Whether the performance is sufficient to support the IPv6-only datacenter scenario has to be tested.

Summary

To summarize this chapter, here are the rules for using integration mechanisms in your high-level plan and deployment strategy:

- Go native IPv6 wherever you can.
- Use tunneling mechanisms only where they are really needed.
- Use translation only if there is no other way.
- Remove all transition mechanisms as soon as you no longer need them.

References

References

Grossetete, Patrick, Ciprian Popoviciu, and Fred Wettling. *Global IPv6 Strategies: From Business Analysis to Operational Planning*. Indianapolis, IN: Cisco Press, 2008.

"Guidelines for the Secure Deployment of IPv6." National Institute of Standards and Technology. *http://csrc.nist.gov/publications/nistpubs/800-119/sp800-119.pdf*.

"Preparing an IPv6 Addressing Plan." RIPE Guide. *http://labs.ripe.net/Members/stef fann/preparing-an-ipv6-addressing-plan*.

RFC 3531: "A Flexible Method for Managing the Assignment of Bits of an IPv6 Address Block." *http://tools.ietf.org/html/rfc3531*.

RFC 5375: "IPv6 Unicast Address Assignment Considerations." *http://tools.ietf.org/html/rfc5375*.

RFC 6052: "IPv6 Addressing of IPv4/IPv6 Translators." *http://tools.ietf.org/html/rfc6052*.

RFC 6144: "Framework for IPv4/IPv6 Translation." *http://tools.ietf.org/html/rfc6144*.

RFC 6177: " IPv6 Address Assignment to End Sites." *http://tools.ietf.org/html/rfc6177*.

RFC 6180: "Guidelines for Using IPv6 Transition Mechanisms during IPv6 Deployment." *http://tools.ietf.org/html/rfc6180*.

"USGv6 Test Methods: General Description and Validation." National Institute of Standards and Technology. *w3.antd.nist.gov/usgv6/NIST-SP-500-273.v2.print.pdf*.

About the Author

Silvia Hagen has been working in the networking industry since 1990. Today she is CEO of Sunny Connection AG in Switzerland and works as a professional consultant and analyst for many midsize and large companies. Her expertise is in IPv6, protocol and performance analysis, and identity management. She is the author of several successful books, including *IPv6 Essentials* (O'Reilly). She has also presented internationally at IPv6 summits, Cisco conferences, Burton Catalyst, Novell BrainShare, NetWare Users International conferences, and universities. She has developed several specialized courses on different topics, including IPv6, and offers them as customized corporate presentations and public courses. She is a member of the International IPv6 Forum and the president of the Swiss IPv6 Council.

Get even more for your money.

Join the O'Reilly Community, and register the O'Reilly books you own. It's free, and you'll get:

- $4.99 ebook upgrade offer
- 40% upgrade offer on O'Reilly print books
- Membership discounts on books and events
- Free lifetime updates to ebooks and videos
- Multiple ebook formats, DRM FREE
- Participation in the O'Reilly community
- Newsletters
- Account management
- 100% Satisfaction Guarantee

Signing up is easy:

1. **Go to: oreilly.com/go/register**
2. **Create an O'Reilly login.**
3. **Provide your address.**
4. **Register your books.**

Note: English-language books only

To order books online:
oreilly.com/store

For questions about products or an order:
orders@oreilly.com

To sign up to get topic-specific email announcements and/or news about upcoming books, conferences, special offers, and new technologies:
elists@oreilly.com

For technical questions about book content:
booktech@oreilly.com

To submit new book proposals to our editors:
proposals@oreilly.com

O'Reilly books are available in multiple DRM-free ebook formats. For more information:
oreilly.com/ebooks

O'REILLY®

Spreading the knowledge of innovators   oreilly.com

The information you need, when and where you need it.

With Safari Books Online, you can:

Access the contents of thousands of technology and business books

- Quickly search over 7000 books and certification guides
- Download whole books or chapters in PDF format, at no extra cost, to print or read on the go
- Copy and paste code
- Save up to 35% on O'Reilly print books
- **New!** Access mobile-friendly books directly from cell phones and mobile devices

Stay up-to-date on emerging topics before the books are published

- Get on-demand access to evolving manuscripts.
- Interact directly with authors of upcoming books

Explore thousands of hours of video on technology and design topics

- Learn from expert video tutorials
- Watch and replay recorded conference sessions

Spreading the knowledge of innovators   safari.oreilly.com